EROICA

EROICA

THE FIRST GREAT ROMANTIC SYMPHONY

JAMES HAMILTON-PATERSON

HEAD of ZEUS

First published in 2016
by Head of Zeus Ltd

Copyright
© James Hamilton-Paterson 2016

1 3 5 7 9 10 8 6 4 2

A CIP catalogue record for this book is available
from the British Library.

ISBN   (HB) 9781784977214
       (E) 9781784977207

Designed and typeset by
Isambard Thomas, London

Colour reproduciton by DawkinsColour

Printed and bound in Spain by Graficas Estella

Head of Zeus Ltd
Clerkenwell House
45–47 Clerkenwell Green
London EC1R 0HT

WWW.HEADOFZEUS.COM

PREVIOUS PAGE

A miniature of Beethoven in
1803 done by the Danish artist
Christian Horneman. It is probably
the most accurate of all the earlier
portraits and Beethoven himself
valued it highly enough to give it to
his old friend from his Bonn days,
Stephan von Breuning.

OVERLEAF

A view of Vienna in 1760 by
Bernardo Bellotto. In the foreground
is the Belvedere with St Stephen's
Cathedral at the painting's centre.
The dominant impression is of
Baroque splendour; unseen is the
squalor and bustle of the distant city,
the vast Austrian Empire's
commercial and artistic hub.

1

INTRODUCTION
& GLOSSARY

For all the fame of Beethoven's Third Symphony, the 'Eroica', each new generation of concertgoers and music-lovers can probably benefit from being reminded of quite what a ground-breaking work it was when first performed in 1805. At that time its immediate claim to notoriety was that it appeared to have rudely broken the mould of the Viennese Classical symphony at a stroke, and in some ways it had. However, it was not merely a musical form that it changed for good. The 'Eroica' also revealed a new and powerful expressiveness of both a personal and a societal kind. Private importuning with appeals to the emotions was to become the staple of the Romantics with whom Beethoven overlapped. But the more public kind of buttonholing achieved by the 'Eroica' and its successors (particularly the Fifth and Ninth Symphonies) seemed to carry an earnest message that was easy to associate with numinous – not to say grandiose – concepts such as Will and Triumph and even the Brotherhood of Man. This was something quite new.

Beethoven himself made explicit the connection between the 'Eroica' and Napoleon Bonaparte, and the symphony does indeed have revolutionary overtones of various kinds. Yet today this seems less important than the effect it has had in the last two centuries on the whole course of Western music. 'Just as France has its Revolution, so Germany has its Beethoven symphonies': thus Robert Schumann in 1839. To Beethoven's symphonies we can directly attribute the modern orchestra and its conductor, the modern concert hall and the modern

concert programme, of which they are still a core element
(one that is much resented in some quarters). How this came
about is worth a closer look.

First, though, it might be useful to put Beethoven's music
and the style he inherited into historical context. No matter
how original a musician he was, he still faced the same basic
problem that any composer of abstract music faced and still
faces: how is he or she to keep it going? This is obviously less
difficult for music that is 'narrative' in the sense of setting a
text, accompanying a film, or representing in sound scenes
such as battles or pastoral landscapes. But in the absence of
such external ways of driving music forward it all becomes
more problematical. For instance, it is well and good to start
with a great tune, but there is a limit to how often it can just be
repeated. It has to *go* somewhere. The question remains: where
next, and why there? One solution discovered centuries ago
was to take the tune and write variations on it, as Beethoven
did in the last movement of the 'Eroica'.

VARIATION FORM

As the name suggests, this involves taking a tune and decorating
or altering it in different ways while still keeping it recognizable.
In earlier times sets of keyboard variations (like some of
Handel's) could be fairly monotonous and conventional. J. S.
Bach's *Goldberg Variations* were probably the first set to show
what could be achieved with the form. In the latter half of the

eighteenth century and with certain exceptions (for example in a number of symphonic and instrumental works by Haydn and Mozart), sets of variations often tended towards salon triviality. After initially writing variations mainly for his own use to show off his skill as a pianist, Beethoven increasingly used the form to express some of his most personal music. In his later use of variations the tune he started with often became harder and harder to recognize as he imaginatively exploited its remoter possibilities.

Apart from variations, what else might drive a piece of music onwards? In the Medieval period when most European music was either ecclesiastical or folksong the problem of the form music might take was presumably less pressing because either words or dancing provided the extra-musical impetus. However, composers who wanted more sophistication to their music than was afforded by the beautiful but wandering and somewhat shapeless unison of Gregorian chant were well aware of the problem of form. Above all, they wanted some interesting harmony. With the late fifteenth-century masses and motets of composers such as Ockeghem, Josquin Desprez and others of the Franco-Flemish school an ingenious style evolved, leading to the great works of Palestrina. This was contrapuntal music of astonishing complexity, often taking a popular tune as its foundation and elaborating it by means of intricate canons and inversions and other devices.

COUNTERPOINT, CANON & FUGUE

Instead of a tune being harmonized *vertically*, with the four 'voices' (soprano, alto, tenor and bass) forming simple chords beneath it as in 'God Save the Queen' or 'Kumbaya', counterpoint has the voices running *horizontally* 'against' (counter) each other. Usually each voice has its own tune, and it is up to the composer's skill to make these individual tunes integrate in a harmonically pleasing way. At any one moment, taken vertically, the voices might not harmonize at all; but the ear expects them to come together shortly and resolve any discords, and it can be immensely pleasing when they do, like any other kind of deferred satisfaction. One of the best-known early examples of this is Thomas Tallis's magnificent motet *Spem in alium*, written in about 1570: a contrapuntal tour de force with forty independent voices.

A special form of counterpoint is canon. 'Frère Jacques' or 'London's Burning' are well-known examples. Both are tunes that can be sung 'vertically' by all four voices at once. On the other hand the voices can also come in independently, contrapuntally, one after the other in any order, with a fixed delay between entries, and still make a harmonious sound, going on and on as long as anyone can bear it because there is no longer any obvious place to stop. It was not for nothing that such canons used to be known as 'rounds' in English. The two examples mentioned above are not very sophisticated. Once again Thomas Tallis supplies a well-known example of something a good deal more beautiful in 'Tallis's Canon', which is usually sung to the Church of England evening hymn 'Glory to Thee my God this night'. Music students were often set the task of composing canons, since it is excellent practice for hearing different voices independently. Bach, Haydn, Mozart and Beethoven all wrote dozens, often to highly dubious or even downright obscene words. (Mozart especially. His canon 'Lick my arse' was eventually published by the German firm Breitkopf as 'Let us be merry'.)

The elaborate use of counterpoint became the basis of the Baroque style that was further developed throughout Europe and essentially lasted until the death of J. S. Bach in 1750. Probably its best-known form is that of the fugue. There are strict fugues and much looser ones, and they can in theory be for any number of independent voices but are mostly written for between two and five. One voice starts out all alone with a basic tune (often only a few notes) known as the subject. When that is finished a second voice comes in with the same subject while the first voice has a counter-subject that goes well with it. Any other voices then join in one by one along the same lines. Together they try to exhaust its musical potential, often by temporarily casting a subject that is in a major key into a minor one and vice versa. (An example of a tune in a major or 'cheerful' key is 'Guide me, oh thou great redeemer' – the 'Bread of Heaven' tune beloved of Welsh rugby fans. In Western music minor keys are generally supposed to sound sadder than major ones. The majority of popular music is in a major key but notable exceptions are the Beatles' 'Eleanor

Rigby' (E minor), Aerosmith's 'Dream On' (F minor) and Led Zeppelin's 'Stairway to Heaven' (A minor).

Fugues vary a good deal according to when and where they were written, as well as whether they are instrumental or choral. A good example of a well-known choral fugue is 'He trusted in God that he would deliver him' in Handel's *Messiah*, where the voices enter in order from bass to soprano. Choral fugues were often more relaxed than instrumental fugues because they were typically composed to create a resounding climax in a cathedral. Instrumental fugues, especially for keyboard, tended to be stricter and more cerebral. Arguably the *ne plus ultra* of this was Bach's *The Art of Fugue*, his last, unfinished major work, which treats a single subject of eleven notes in fifteen separate fugues plus four canons during which the subject is inverted, played backwards, inverted *and* played backwards, expanded and contracted and generally worked over in different rhythms in an astonishing display of contrapuntal mastery.

Despite the Baroque style steadily going out of fashion in the early decades of the eighteenth century, fugues or the fugal style persisted, especially in the conservative realm of Church music. Also, writing fugues was an essential part of every musician's training (and still is in many university music courses) as the tried-and-tested way of achieving discipline and competence in the independent handling of voices and instruments. As we shall see, composers such as Haydn, Mozart and Beethoven all had reasons for using the fugal style in their secular music, as have many composers since. Often they would get an element of seriousness by *fugato* (i.e. 'fugued') passages that sounded learned but stopped well short of being complete, worked-out fugues. There are happy instances of this in both the first and last movements of the 'Eroica'.

GALANT STYLE, SONATA FORM & CLASSICAL STYLE

By 1750 popular taste had long since wearied of this 'learned' style and wanted something altogether lighter and more tuneful – a taste that had grown from the early eighteenth century as the music of Vivaldi, Pergolesi and other Italians welled upwards into northern climes like cheerful spring sap. Even Carl Philipp Emanuel, Bach's celebrated eldest son and chief exponent of the emotional style known as *Empfindsamkeit* or 'sentimentality', would refer to his father privately but fondly as 'The Old Wig'. A *galant* style evolved, full of endless minuets and dance tunes of the kind that often overlapped with what in German-speaking countries was sometimes known as *Tafelmusik*. This was music a small ensemble of instruments could play at balls and banquets: a sort of eighteenth-century muzak for easy listening or else as background music (much like the meaningless 'beat' track laid behind many of today's radio announcements such as weather forecasts). *Galant* music was often precious and unmemorable; its short-winded tunes often ornamented with a lot of empty twiddles. It was of no help to serious composers looking for a way to give their music impetus. In operas and oratorios words still carried their own onward momentum, of course; but in the absence of being able to rely on unfashionable contrapuntal devices composers needed to find another motivating force able to drive a piece of 'serious' abstract music forward in a way that sounded purposeful and also made musical sense. This problem was solved by the gradual coalescence of various elements into what became established as 'sonata form'.

Sonata form was never a structure as rigid as, say, that of a Shakespearean sonnet or most fugues, but it did normally adhere to a pattern that broadly went as follows. The opening tune would be followed by a move out of the home key, or tonic, into the dominant. (The dominant is the fifth note above the tonic and in traditional harmony is thought of as being the one that most urgently requires 'resolution' back to the tonic. On the piano, if the tonic is C the dominant is G. Imagine you are singing 'Cockles and Mussels': 'In Dublin's fair city/Where girls are so pretty/I first set my eyes on sweet Molly Mal*one*.' On the last syllable of 'Malone' you are in the dominant. It makes you want to return to the tonic with 'As she wheeled her wheelbarrow. . .' and stay there for the rest of the verse).

A change of key was already a recognized way not just of avoiding monotony but of pushing the music forward. It was a tried and trusted method and still remains so. At its most blatantly feeble the device was common in pop music of the 1960s, typically after a couple of verses when with a sort of gear-change the entire tune would be shifted up a semitone (sometimes more than once), usually with no attempt to 'resolve' the song back into the key in which it had begun.

In sonata form, once the dominant key was reached an entirely new tune would be introduced, often with subsidiary motifs or tunelets. That section typically closed in the same dominant key with a double bar-line that by a convention inherited from the Baroque 'da capo' aria meant the players went back and repeated the section from the beginning. When this repeat was done there followed a development section where the various tunes were played around with, often involving excursions through different keys and with varied devices, before the music was gradually (and often ingeniously) brought back to the 'home' tonic key where the main tunes were recapitulated either in their original form or else somewhat altered as though bruised or enhanced by their passage through the development. Sometimes a little coda would be tagged on at the end to sum things up and bring the movement to a close.

In this way the whole progress of the music in sonata form was really predicated on getting back to the right key. In abbreviated schematic form: the 'home' key was established at the outset, lost, then considerably dishevelled before satisfaction came from regaining it. It was something like a musical version of farce, which starts with a well-ordered world that is swiftly turned upside-down by misunderstandings and seemingly logical absurdities before order is at last restored, to the audience's relief.

CLASSICAL STYLE

Although 'classical' as an adjective is still sometimes used today to distinguish 'serious' or 'art' music from more 'popular' genres, Classical style (sometimes subdivided as Viennese Classical style) has generally come to mean the sort of music written largely in the second half of the eighteenth century. This is fuzzy at its early end with the overlap of Baroque musicians such as Bach and Handel (who died in 1750 and 1759 respectively) and likewise at the later end as composers such as Beethoven and Schubert overlapped with Romantic musicians including Chopin and Schumann (both born in 1810). Since for most of this time Vienna was the focal city of European music, if only for the sheer number of first-rate musicians who either worked in the city or came directly under its influence, the concept of the Viennese Classics has become shorthand for the predominant musical style of the period encompassed by Haydn (1732–1809), Mozart (1756–1791) and Beethoven (1770–1827).

Sonata form was the lifeblood of the Classical style. It was wonderfully adaptable. It lent itself to considerable compression for short pieces but equally to more leisurely treatment for grander works. With an infinite number of minor deviations at the whim of the composer, sonata form constituted the predominant basic structure of Classical music (especially as exemplified by keyboard sonatas) from roughly 1740 to 1820. At its most humdrum it became formulaic, but good composers discovered it had immense flexibility and it became the norm

for nearly all first movements as well as for much else across a
wide range of music, from little flute sonatas to string quartets
to symphonies. Despite the enormous strain Beethoven was
to place it under in the 'Eroica' and later works, it is still easy
to detect the form's influence well into the Romantic period of
Schumann and Chopin, even right through to Brahms – in
other words practically until the end of the nineteenth century.
At that point conventional harmony, already painfully stretched
by composers such as Richard Strauss, was finally destroyed by
the twelve-tone music of Schoenberg, Berg and Webern. Once
the importance of key had been abolished, sonata form lost its
mainspring. But in the years of its supremacy its success was a
tribute to its efficacy in giving forward momentum to a piece
of otherwise abstract music.

2

THE BOY FROM BONN

It used to be customary to present Beethoven's family background and boyhood almost as a contrast to Mozart's, as though to show how a heroic genius could dispense with the advantages of being a child prodigy painstakingly groomed by a father who was both an accomplished professional musician and extremely ambitious for his son. In fact Beethoven's father Johann was also a professional musician (although much less accomplished than Leopold Mozart) and ambitious enough for his son occasionally to shave a year or two off the boy's age just as Leopold did with Wolfgang. The market for child musical celebs was very lively in the latter half of the eighteenth century.

Young Beethoven was certainly not a child prodigy to the same degree as Mozart or Mendelssohn, but it was obvious early on that he had quite exceptional musical talent. Music did after all run in the family. His grandfather Ludwig (1712–1773), who died when Beethoven was not quite three, came from what today is Belgium and was a trained singer who accepted a post in the Elector of Cologne's chapel at his court in Bonn. That he must also have been a thorough musician as well as having a notable voice is proved by his subsequent appointment there as Kapellmeister in 1761 with responsibility to supervise all the court's music. Such a post normally went to a composer, which the elder Ludwig never was.

Ludwig's son Johann (1740–1792) also joined the Elector's chapel as a singer, first as a boy and then staying on as a tenor.

Johann had enough ability on both the violin and the harpsichord to give basic lessons to eke out his stipend but his musical talents were much more modest than his father's. He married in 1767, and his second surviving son, Ludwig, was born in December 1770. Two younger brothers also survived, Carl and Johann, both of whom were to figure prominently in Beethoven's later life.

Having spotted Ludwig's early talent Beethoven's father did his best to foster it by giving him basic keyboard and violin lessons. The boy was then sent to various teachers in Bonn and gave his first concert when he was seven, playing 'various concertos and trios', which surely argues rapid progress. But under his father's bullying the boy Beethoven was soon as overworked as the boy Mozart had been some fifteen years earlier, but with none of that little showman's satin suits, miniature court dress and periwigs. On the contrary, as a child of what the current British euphemism would call a 'troubled family' young Ludwig bore clear signs of neglect, under-nourishment and, on occasion, welts and bruises from his father's beatings. His younger brothers, showing no signs of musical precocity, probably escaped the worst consequences of their father's ambitiousness. Outside the house Johann was convivial and not unpopular but occasionally showed the effects of heavy drinking, his voice and court attendance already beginning to suffer.

Maria, the boys' mother, was a kindly soul, although she could flare up suddenly with formidable outbursts of temper,

as could all the Beethovens. Somehow she dealt with her difficult husband, but trying to hold the family together was taxing and at school her children were noted for being generally unkempt and grubby. Ludwig's formal education never progressed even as far as Gymnasium level (secondary school, in British terms) but stopped at Bonn's Tirocinium, or primary school, from which he was removed in 1781 in order to concentrate on music. He was not quite eleven. Years later one of his fellow pupils at the Tirocinium remembered the boy they called either 'Luis' or 'der Spagnol', the Spaniard, because of his dark complexion and haughtiness:

Apparently his mother was already dead at the time, for Luis v. B. was distinguished by uncleanliness, negligence, etc. Not a sign was to be discovered of that spark of genius which glowed so brilliantly in him afterwards.[1]

In fact poor Maria was not dead, merely ill with the early stages of tuberculosis and ever more exhausted with maintaining the household and keeping her three children fed and presentable.

In leaving school so young Ludwig was not exceptional for the times. Eleven was considered an appropriate age for a boy in a needy family to get out into the world and become apprenticed to a worthwhile trade, earning being much preferred to learning. Ludwig self-selected for the trade of music: he was as brilliant at that as he was backward in such basic skills as even the most elementary mathematics. In the vast archive of manuscripts, notes, diaries, conversation books and scribbles he was to leave behind are various touching efforts at accountancy that betray this lack. He never learned how to multiply, for example. If he needed to multiply a sum of money by forty he wrote it out forty times and added the column up, not always reaching the same total twice running.

The first music teacher to have a far-reaching influence on the young Beethoven was Christian Gottlob Neefe, who was appointed court organist in Bonn in 1781. It was Neefe who introduced the boy to J. S. Bach's *48 Preludes and Fugues* in all the keys at a time when the Baroque master's music had fallen out of fashion. In the thirty-one years since Bach's death, his legacy was kept alive by a comparative handful of enthusiasts. (It would be almost another half-century before Mendelssohn resurrected the *St Matthew Passion* from total obscurity to astonish audiences then firmly in music's Romantic age and re-establish Bach in his rightful place.) Bach's '*48*' proved the perfect grounding for a more advanced piano technique, as it did for Beethoven's own later and highly idiosyncratic brand of fugue. At eleven Ludwig was already accomplished enough to act as Neefe's deputy as court organist, and Neefe himself admiringly described his prize pupil in a magazine article as being a skilled keyboard player and sight-reader, as well as having had a composition published. This was a set of nine piano variations on a march by the minor composer Ernst Christoph Dressler. (In the context of the 'Eroica' Symphony, with its famous funeral march in C minor, it is a curious coincidence that the theme of Dressler's the boy Beethoven should have chosen for his first published piece was also a funeral march in C minor). Neefe's article ended: 'This young genius deserves help to enable him to travel. He would surely become a second Wolfgang Amadeus Mozart if he were to continue as he has begun.'[2]

Before he turned thirteen Beethoven had risen to be deputy continuo player in the Elector Maximilian Friedrich's orchestra with three published sonatas judiciously dedicated to his employer. The continuo player's chief task had long been that of accompanying from the keyboard the singers of recitatives in operas and cantatas. By this time the traditional harpsichord was slowly being replaced by the fortepiano, and in those pre-conductor days the continuo player also helped keep the orchestra together. The job was a considerable test of sight-reading from scores as well as time-keeping and would have been invaluable for familiarizing Beethoven with ensemble playing. The following year the Elector died and was succeeded by Archduke Maximilian Francis, Empress Maria Theresa's youngest son. His title might have been Archbishop and Elector-Spiritual of Cologne, but his court was in Bonn, as it had been for all the Electors of Cologne for centuries. The new Elector was keen to make Bonn an artistic centre to rival Vienna, the city of his birth. Knowing his keen interest in music, Neefe put forward his prize pupil for the post of assistant court organist, to which the thirteen-year-old Beethoven was duly appointed at a salary of 150 gulden. The relief in the Beethoven household must have been immense. The boy was making good. It is hard to imagine that Johann went to bed sober that night. The Elector soon began to take a personal interest in his young organist, recognizing the ferocious nature of the boy's talent.

From Beethoven's point of view the next few years were perfect for his musical education in that his duties were not onerous and left him with plenty of time for perfecting his keyboard technique. Better still, he had the court orchestra from which to learn the range of each instrument, its uses, its tonal limitations and ability to blend in or stand out in an ensemble. From his father he had learned the basics of violin technique and turned himself into a viola player good enough to take his place in the opera orchestra, but he was never a natural string player. Such skills were merely what any practical musician picked up along the way. Haydn, for example, claimed to be able to play any instrument in the orchestra, none brilliantly but all of them quite well enough for him to be able to deputize at the desk of an absent player.

Two scholars who wrote outstanding Beethoven biographies in the early 1930s, Marion M. Scott (*Beethoven*) and Richard Specht (*Bildnis Beethovens*), referred to an incident from this period that later biographers have ignored, although this might be for lack of a reliable source. In Marion Scott's version the story goes:

Beethoven, during the course of his duties. . . had to accompany on the piano those portions of the Lamentations of Jeremiah which are sung on a reciting note in Holy Week. In Holy Week, March 1785, the singer was Ferdinand Heller, an excellent musician who, when Beethoven asked leave to try to put him off his note, assented very readily. [The boy], while persistently striking the reciting note with one finger, improvised such daring harmonic excursions in the accompaniment that Heller became too bewildered to find the closing cadence. . . The musicians of the chapel were dumbfounded at Beethoven's skill, Heller was furious to the extent of complaining to the Elector, and the triumphant youngster was 'very graciously reprimanded' by that exalted person.[3]

The composer's grandfather, Ludwig van Beethoven, at the age of sixty-one in a portrait by Amelius Radoux, a fellow-Belgian. It was painted in 1773 when Ludwig was Kapellmeister at the Elector's court in Bonn. Earlier that year the old musician had had a stroke and he would die on Christmas Eve.

The story sounds likely enough since there are plenty of well-attested accounts from only very little later of Beethoven's prodigious skill as an improviser, especially when challenged to work from a mere handful of notes. It also contains a plausible germ of the arrogance that was to remain a characteristic of most of the subsequent musical challenges he accepted, especially later in Vienna where competitions between keyboard players were keenly fought.

At the age of fourteen Beethoven published the first compositions to have his precocious personal stamp: the three Piano Quartets WoO 36 (a great many of his early and uncollected works were marked thus as works without an opus number). The music inevitably shows the influence of Mozart, partly because he was the composer who most inspired the young Beethoven but also because each quartet was modelled on one of Mozart's violin sonatas. Despite that, these compositions betray surprising individuality and a depth of controlled feeling quite unexpected in anyone so young. Beethoven obviously wrote these quartets with himself as pianist in mind, and as such they are a testimonial to the keyboard technique he had acquired, since they are much more demanding for the pianist than Mozart's violin sonatas. The second movement of the E flat major Quartet (WoO 36 No. 1) is not only in the stormy, passionate mode that later became one of his trademarks when he set up in Vienna; it is in the tonic minor – the rare key of E flat minor, the six flats presenting difficulties to all the players: to the strings in terms of intonation and to the pianist because having to deal with so many black keys was seldom encountered outside Bach's '*48*' (a difficulty related to that of tuning keyboard instruments in the remoter keys). Beethoven's familiarity with Bach's work surely facilitated this logical but unusual choice.

All three of these piano quartets show clear pointers towards later works. In particular he was to adapt the slow movement of No. 3 in C major ten years later as the *Adagio* of the first of his thirty-two piano sonatas, the F minor, Op. 2 No. 1; while a G minor passage in the quartet's first movement was to re-appear in the Piano Sonata in C major, Op. 2 No. 3. More importantly in the present context, though, in two of these quartets there are remarkable suggestions in embryonic form of the 'Prometheus' theme that in fifteen and more years' time Beethoven was to use in four separate works, culminating with the last movement of the 'Eroica'.[*]

––––––––––

[*] See Appendix, p. 183.

THE BOY FROM BONN

Were these prophetic hints, not yet fully realized, of a tune that was to become famous in twenty years' time or were they just a musical commonplace, more fragments of a tune than a tune itself? Musicologists have also pointed to two of Muzio Clementi's piano sonatas as possible influences for this theme, especially his F minor Sonata, Op. 13 No. 6, dating from 1784.[4] Its last movement begins with the first few notes of the 'Prometheus' theme, albeit in a minor key, but later in the movement it appears in the major and does sound convincingly similar. Clementi was perhaps the first virtuoso of the early piano, and later on his numerous sonatas undoubtedly had some influence on Beethoven, who certainly had copies in his library as an adult and also had business relations with the Italian. But that Beethoven could have seen a sonata written only the year before his own piano quartets seems doubtful, and in any case too much can be made of these apparent musical cross-references and presagings.

A handful of notes that might have foreshadowed an entire later tune seem of little significance, particularly as Beethoven never felt himself remotely challenged by Clementi either as a performer or as a composer. Unknown to his fourteen-year-old self in 1785, of course, it was precisely the use and expansion of such motivic fragments that was to become the trademark of his maturity. At the time, composers such as Mozart and Haydn tended to favour self-contained tunes they would develop in ways that usually left them still identifiable. Beethoven was to invent a method of either starting with bald rhythmic motifs (like the opening of the Fifth Symphony) that could be expanded into tunes, or else doing the opposite: starting with a tune and reducing it to its component parts (as in the last movement of the Eighth). These techniques became a salient feature of his mature compositions and not least of the 'Eroica' Symphony. Whatever its origins, this particular germ of the later 'Prometheus' tune clearly had a long genesis.

Hearing these early quartets, no musician in the new Elector's court in Bonn could have been in any further doubt about young Beethoven's great gifts and promise. Archduke Maximilian took particular notice of him, not merely as an ornament to his court but as a potential inheritor of Mozart's laurels. This interest in his promising organist's future was all of a piece with his plan to convert Bonn from an ecclesiastical Rhenish backwater into a seat of the arts and learning. He was very much a man of the Enlightenment, encouraging science and laying out botanical gardens, opening a public reading room in the library of his palace and inaugurating the new university his predecessor had planned. Ignorant of the awful changes that lay in wait for Bonn at the hands of Napoleon following the French Revolution of 1789, for a few brief but exciting years the city basked in a springlike regeneration that attracted artists and intellectuals. It was this period and this progressive atmosphere that Beethoven was to retain for the rest of his life as an image of civilized orderliness that epitomized his birthplace, his locus of homesickness.

Beethoven the teenager might have been ill educated in a

formal sense and often socially uncouth, but in other respects he was the beneficiary of a good deal of extra-musical intellectual stimulus. His teacher and mentor, Christian Neefe, was a creature of the Enlightenment with pronounced egalitarian views that verged on the mystical. He was a Freemason as well as a member of the more secretive and politically radical Bavarian Order of Illuminati. Such interests were very much in the spirit of the times. Many of the leading artists and intellectuals of the day were Masons, from Benjamin Franklin and George Washington in America to Goethe and Frederick the Great, not to mention Gluck, Mozart and Haydn closer to home. The playwright Gotthold Ephraim Lessing, author of *Nathan the Wise* (1779), was also a Mason. *Nathan* made a powerful plea for the peaceful co-existence of Christianity, Judaism and Islam, and this parable of the brotherhood of man was already famous throughout Europe. He described the central belief of Freemasonry thus:

By the exercise of Brotherly Love we are taught to regard the whole human species as one family, the high and the low, the rich and the poor, created by one Almighty Being and sent into the world for the aid, support and protection of each other. On these principles Masonry unites men of every country, sect and opinion, and by its dictates conciliates true friendship among those who might otherwise have remained at a distance.[1]

From Neefe and others of his circle Beethoven would have heard such ideas and no doubt internalized them as a vindication of his own humble origins, together with the

Joseph Haydn in 1791. This portrait of Europe's most famous composer at the age of fi fty-eight was painted in London by Thomas Hardy shortly after Haydn's arrival on the fi rst of two immensely successful visits to England. In Vienna the following year Beethoven, then newly arrived from his native Bonn, was to become Haydn's less than model pupil.

implied reassurance that lowly birth was no bar to future greatness. From its first publication and wide circulation in 1786, Schiller's poem 'Ode to Joy' must also have deeply impressed the teenager. Although Schiller was not himself a Freemason, many of the poem's sentiments (*Alle Menschen werden Brüder*: 'All men shall be brothers') perfectly echoed the Masonic ideals. Indeed, once Beethoven had finally settled in Vienna in the next decade he decided he would set the poem to music, although it was thirty years before he got around to it for the last movement of the Ninth Symphony. It might seem surprising that Beethoven never became a Freemason himself: he was to have many friends in Vienna who were, several of them aristocrats. But he was never a joiner. Constitutionally unclubbable as Beethoven was, it is impossible to visualize him as a member of any organization. Any oaths and rules in his life were exclusively his own. Despite all his invocations of the brotherhood of man, he powerfully felt himself a loner, often belligerently so.

Meanwhile he concentrated on honing his piano technique and was giving lessons to various aristocratic children in Bonn until, in the late spring of 1787, Archduke Maximilian sent for him and announced he was sending him to Vienna, all expenses paid. The sixteen-year-old travelled alone and it is not known exactly what the purpose of the trip was. Since the Archduke was himself a keen amateur musician and his brother Joseph II was Holy Roman Emperor in Vienna, there was no one in that city to whom Beethoven might not have been given an introduction, and doubtless he left home with a sheaf of appropriate letters with impressive wax seals. Certainly he longed to meet Mozart and Haydn, although at that time Haydn was an almost permanent fixture at Eszterháza Palace, about fifty miles south-east of Vienna just over today's Hungarian border, where he was Kapellmeister, seldom coming to Vienna except for short visits at Christmas.

In the event Beethoven did meet the rushed and preoccupied Mozart and played for him – or so goes the legend, since there is no reliable record of this visit. Tradition also has Mozart turning to some others as Beethoven was playing to say, 'Keep your eyes on that boy – some day he'll give the world something to talk about', in the approved way by which legendary figures endorse their worthy successors, just as Haydn had the young Mozart. It makes a story. But nothing else is known about this

visit, which was anyway cut short after less than a fortnight when news reached Beethoven that his mother Maria was now mortally ill. He returned post-haste to Bonn, arriving somewhat ill himself after the days of travel in lurching coaches over appalling roads. He nursed her until she died barely two weeks later, aged forty. Deeply attached to her as he was, Beethoven was bereft, saying he had lost his best friend. (Her gravestone is marked by her famous son's words: *Sie war mir eine so gute liebenswürdige Mutter, meine beste Freundin*). He was old enough to recognize the struggle she had had to make a home for him, his two brothers and an afterthought – a one-year-old baby sister – in a household in which Johann had lately been a barely effectual husband.

In this way at the age of sixteen Ludwig became the family's main breadwinner, Johann having already begun his decline into alcoholism, eventually losing his employment at court because his singing voice had deteriorated so badly. Many of the family's possessions were pawned. The baby girl died in November. Two years later Johann was sacked, and Ludwig petitioned to be recognized as the de facto head of the Beethoven family. This was granted, so the eldest son's moral duty became also a legal one. His father had become an embarrassment, and Beethoven's closest friend Stephan von Breuning later remembered an occasion when Ludwig had furiously intervened to prevent his incapably drunk father from being arrested in the street.

There is no doubt that at dark periods at this stage of his

life Beethoven relied heavily on his friendships to save him from utter despondency. He had long given piano lessons to the slightly younger children of the large and well-to-do von Breuning family, and the widowed Frau von Breuning, a most intelligent lady who recognized young Ludwig's exceptional talent and understood his black moods, was motherly and infallibly kind. Another lifetime friend of Ludwig's from this period was Franz Wegeler, a young doctor who would marry one of the von Breuning girls and eventually write a biography of Beethoven. The young musician might have been a loner, not to say impossibly difficult on occasion, but it is clear he must have had something lovable about him that was capable of being coaxed into lasting friendships. It is anyone's guess whether Beethoven would have survived this grim period in his life without his supportive friends.

Another of his long-term friendships from this period was with Count Ferdinand von Waldstein, some eight years older than Beethoven and a keen amateur musician as well as a close friend of the Elector. Waldstein gave Beethoven a piano, and in due time Beethoven dedicated his Piano Sonata in C major, Op. 53, to him, the work every pianist knows as the 'Waldstein'. As the 1780s ended Beethoven was busy refining his piano technique, acquiring a working knowledge of the orchestra and composing numerous works varied enough to show his competence in different forms. Then suddenly, in February 1790, the news came that Joseph II, the Elector's older brother, had died in Vienna.

Joseph II, like his Prussian contemporary Frederick the Great, had been an admirer of Voltaire and Rousseau and the Enlightenment generally. Despite commanding the Holy Roman Empire he had privately hankered after such things as a secular state and the abolition of serfdom. His mother, the Empress Maria Theresa, had summarily banned the Jesuits from the Empire in 1773, causing uproar in the Vatican. While he himself remained a Catholic, Joseph went on to grant religious autonomy to Protestants and Jews. Although never joining a lodge, he was also amiably inclined towards Freemasonry.

Joseph II was musical, a great admirer of Mozart and especially of his operas. It was he who commissioned *Die Entführung aus dem Serail* in German rather than in the usual French or Italian, and in Vienna this break with tradition was welcomed as refreshingly nationalist. However, Joseph's basic attitude was less revolutionary than reformist. Frederick the Great had proclaimed that a monarch was not the absolute master of the state but only its first servant. Joseph, as an enlightened despot, might have aspired to this ideal but in the event merely discovered how little power some servants actually wielded. He succeeded in changing very little of the Austrian state, finding himself opposed at every turn by the dead weight of the Church and the conservatism of the aristocracy, the military and the imperial bureaucracy. He tried to change too many things too quickly in the face of powerful men and institutions with too much to lose. Ironically, having been known as 'the people's emperor', he wound up considerably more disliked than loved. Ill and alone and facing revolt on all sides, he asked that his own sad epitaph should be: 'Here lies Joseph II, who failed in all he undertook.' To this day the humble copper sarcophagus he lies in is in stark contrast to the monstrous elaborations in bronze that lie around him in Vienna's Imperial Crypt, the *Kaisergruft*.

At the time, though, Joseph's progressive ideas were widely celebrated beyond the Austrian Empire's boundaries, and when news of his death reached his brother the Elector in Bonn the twenty-year-old Beethoven was given two weeks to write a commemorative cantata. This, the best work of all the composer's early Bonn period, was never performed, probably because it was not finished in time but also on account of its difficulties. For a first attempt at a big choral work with full orchestra it is much better than commendable and full of ambitious and effective writing. The impressively solemn C minor opening strikes a note of distilled sorrow that is strangely personal and affecting for what was, after all, a commissioned occasional piece. The Elector's own sadness at the loss of his brother must have pervaded his court. A similar fate befell the cantata Beethoven then wrote to celebrate the accession of Joseph's successor, his brother Leopold II. The sumptuous orchestration of both these early compositions shows the influence of contemporary French composers such as Le

OVERLEAF
The arrival of Prince Maximilian Franz at the residence of the Elector of Bonn in October 1780, as painted by Johann Franz Rousseau. Prince Maximilian was visiting as the appointed successor to the Electorate. It was as the Elector of Bonn after 1784 that he took the young Beethoven under his wing and gave him appointments at court.

Sueur, Méhul and Gossec, all of whom were busily writing imposing celebratory music at the behest of the Revolution's new institutions.

Thereafter the Elector redoubled his efforts to recruit first-rate musicians for his court orchestra, and soon it was being spoken of as rivalling the famous orchestra at Mannheim. All the players wore scarlet uniforms trimmed abundantly with gold. At last, as a violist, the ex-urchin Beethoven was clad in splendid livery. Better still, he was now valued as easily the best pianist in Bonn and far beyond. Karl Junker, a visiting chaplain who was also a keen amateur musician, referred to him as 'the dear, good Bethofen [*sic*]'. He not only heard Beethoven play but gave him a theme on which to extemporize and spoke of Beethoven as an 'amiable, light-hearted man', praising him for the

almost inexhaustible wealth of ideas, the altogether characteristic style of expression in his playing, and the great execution he displays. . . Yet he is exceedingly modest and free from all pretensions. . . His style of treating his instrument is so different from that usually adopted that it impresses one with the idea that by a path of his own discovery he has attained that height of excellence whereon he now stands.[6]

In December 1790 the Elector's orchestra feted Haydn as he passed through Bonn on the way to England for his first visit. On his return in July 1792 the orchestra gave him a celebratory breakfast by the Rhine at Godesberg, a few miles upstream. It is still uncertain whether it was on this occasion or the earlier one that Beethoven showed the great man one of his compositions – very probably the *Cantata on the Death of Joseph II* – and was no doubt pleased when, according to Wegeler, he was 'encouraged to further study'. But certainly on this second visit it was planned that Beethoven should go to Vienna to study with Haydn and then accompany him to England for the great man's second visit to London, for which Haydn had been contracted by the Bonn-born impresario Johann Peter Salomon. Haydn was privately toying with the idea of staying permanently in England, so warm and lucrative had his reception been there, and it turned out that Beethoven too was thinking seriously about a career in London. The evidence for this is a poem in his *Stammbuch* (commonplace book) by another of the von Breuning brothers, Christoph, dated 19 November 1792:

See! The shady grove, which entices the singer
hasten then without delay
over the surging sea
where a more beauteous grove offers you its shade
and a bard [Salomon] *stretches out his hand to you in friendship,*
who from our fields
fled to Albion's protection.
There let thy song ring loudly and victorious,
let it ring wildly through the grove, across the waves of the sea
to those fields
whence thou hast fled with joy.[7]

In the same commonplace book is Count Waldstein's more famous farewell to his younger friend:

Dear Beethowen! [sic]
You are now going to Vienna in fulfilment of a wish that has for so long been thwarted. The genius of Mozart still mourns and weeps the death of its pupil. It has found a refuge in the inexhaustible Hayden [sic], but no occupation; through him it desires once more to find a union with someone. Through your unceasing diligence, receive Mozart's spirit from the hands of Hayden.

     Your true friend Waldstein.
     Bonn, the 29th Oct. 1792 [8]

In this way Beethoven finally left Bonn for Vienna, and possibly also for England, in early November. It was as well for him, because Bonn was about to be overtaken by political events that had looked increasingly menacing ever since 1789. Even as he left, the French army was closing in on Mainz and Limburg. In France itself the monarchy of a thousand years' standing had just been abolished, and Louis XIV had been arrested, tried and found guilty of high treason (to be guillotined the following January as 'Citizen Louis Capet'). Joseph II's sister, Marie Antoinette, had been in prison in Paris since the Revolution, and another of her late brother's mortified self-accusations of failure had been over the botched attempt to rescue her (she would herself be guillotined in October 1793).

    The boy from Bonn finally arrived in Vienna in November 1792. The deal he had with the Elector was that with the Elector's financial help he would stay and study in Vienna for an unspecified period before returning to his service in Bonn. (Beethoven had presumably kept to himself his intention of defecting to England in case the plan didn't come off.) Two days after Beethoven's twenty-second birthday in December, the news reached him of his father's death. Worse, it turned out Johann had managed to embezzle the money Ludwig had carefully arranged for his younger brothers. He also discovered that the 400 florins he was expecting as a full year's stipend from the Elector to get him settled in the city turned out to be a mere 100 for the first quarter, and by June the following year the stipend itself had dried up entirely because of the Elector's own worsening financial state. Eighteen months after Beethoven's departure Elector Maximilian Francis's reign over Bonn and his adjacent territory came to an end when he fled the advance of the French army that soon annexed the entire left bank of the Rhine. An era had come to an end. Bonn's university was shut down, a 'Freedom Tree' was planted in the market square and the *Code Napoléon* adopted as civil law. The Elector retreated to the city of his birth, Vienna, where he died in 1801 at the age of forty-five, ill and grotesquely fat. Beethoven had planned to dedicate his first symphony gratefully to the man in whose employ he had learned his trade and come of age as a composer and performer, but the Archduke was dead before it could be finished.

3

VIENNA

Strapped for cash but with letters of introduction to some powerful aristocratic contacts and the priceless calling card of his brilliance as a pianist, Beethoven at once began his studies with Haydn. They did not go well. The famous old composer was soon to refer to him with a mixture of amusement and sarcasm as 'The Grand Mogul' to describe his young pupil's manner. Although well able to judge his pupil's musical brilliance, Haydn noted that Beethoven lacked both discipline and a knowledge of counterpoint. Beethoven was outwardly respectful but evidently felt there was not much he could learn from a man whose heyday had surely passed (he was quite wrong there; Haydn had some of his greatest music still to write) and who anyway represented a style of music from which he needed to liberate himself.

For his part the unhappily married and childless Haydn had probably hoped this young genius from Bonn might treat him affectionately as a father figure. Beethoven could certainly be excused for being disillusioned with father–son relationships; but his disenchantment had left him not the slightest insight into their dynamics, a lack tragically evidenced towards the end of his life when he himself tried to be a surrogate father to his young nephew Karl. What neither Haydn nor Beethoven can have realized was that in a musical sense Haydn *was* a father figure to his begrudging student. His fame was Europe-wide and secure; his immense reputation cast a deep shadow out of which Beethoven longed to step without knowing how. It was to be many years before he managed it.

OVERLEAF
The Viennese palace of the Lobkowitz family in 1805, from a coloured engraving by Vincenz Reim. Two years younger than Beethoven and a keen musician himself, Prince Lobkowitz became one of the composer's most loyal and long-suffering patrons. The palace remained in the Lobkowitz family's possession until 1980 and is today the Austrian Theatre Museum.

The old composer meanwhile was long-suffering, genuinely kind and proud of his impoverished pupil who could afford to pay him only pennies compared with the guinea per lesson that Haydn had been earning in London. His haughty student criticized him behind his back for not correcting his exercises with the attention he felt was his due. The truth was that Haydn was preoccupied with writing the music he had promised he would bring back to London for Salomon's new season. At any rate in mid-January 1794 he left for England without Beethoven.

Beethoven's financial state at this time was still miserable, as were his lodgings, but he had put up with it mostly because he always imagined (he *was* still in his early twenties) that once he was in London where the streets were surely paved with gold he would make plenty of money. With the failure of that scheme, though, and in addition to taking counterpoint lessons from the Kapellmeister at St Stephen's, Johann Albrechtsberger (lessons that went little better than those with Haydn), he concentrated on acquiring patrons among the nobility. This he accomplished remarkably easily, not only as a pupil of the celebrated Haydn but because of his connections through men such as the Elector Maximilian Francis and Count Waldstein. But his real calling card was the reputation he was making for his sensational piano playing. Nearly all the early concerts he gave were not public in the modern sense but took place in the salons and music rooms of the nobility and grandees, attended by small numbers of discerning listeners.

The short, dark-complexioned young firebrand from Bonn was soon recognized as a musician quite out of the ordinary, and aristocratic sons and daughters came to hear him and begged for lessons.

In particular, his powers of improvisation soon became legendary. If they also contained an element of pugnaciousness it was partly because that was his character, but it was also because improvising always implied a challenge. In effect it meant inventing a composition on the spot, often on a subject supplied by one of his audience, in a way that made for coherent listening with plenty of showmanship thrown in. As the de facto capital of European music, Vienna was full of highly accomplished musicians from all over the Habsburg Empire, including many well-known pianists, all of whom had their champions. It was a highly competitive musical scene, and by no means always good natured. One famous incident took place at a party in Prince Lobkowitz's palace. Lobkowitz was by then one of Beethoven's patrons, and the party he threw was in honour of Ignaz Pleyel, a man thirteen years older than Beethoven. Pleyel's latest quartets were played, after which the Prince called on Beethoven himself to play, which Beethoven clearly resented. He walked to the piano with bad grace, on the way snatching up the second violinist's part of Pleyel's last quartet, which he then slammed upside-down on the piano's music stand and began to improvise. Carl Czerny, an outstanding pianist himself, described what followed:

He had never been heard to improvise more brilliantly, with more originality and splendour than on this evening. But for the entire improvisation there ran through its middle voices, like a thread or cantus firmus, the notes – in themselves utterly insignificant – which he found on the random page of the quartet he had grabbed and on which he built up the most daring melodies and harmonies in the most brilliant concerto style. At the end poor old Pleyel could only show his amazement by kissing Beethoven's hands.[1]

All the same, Beethoven's piano-playing style, invariably praised for its astonishing technique, was not always preferred to those favouring the earlier style of the Viennese school of Mozart and Haydn. The piano was in a state of rapid development at that time, and instruments varied considerably. They also bore scant resemblance to the modern piano with its vastly greater volume of sound over a much wider range of notes. In Beethoven's boyhood fortepianos were still only patchily available, and his early Bonn works would often have been played on a harpsichord. When he reached Vienna he discovered that Viennese pianos were extremely light in touch, with little sustaining power. Consequently their sound died quite quickly, which was good for a slightly superficial or tinkly style of rapid playing but less good for smoothly sustained slow passages. Mozart had been praised by many for the speed and clarity of his scales and passagework. But Mozart was dead – and Beethoven had famously disparaged his playing as 'choppy' (he heard him play on his brief visit to Vienna in 1787). Beethoven's own speciality – apart from the unequalled rapidity of his double trills, runs and skips – was his slow legato playing and richness of tone. This demanded not only a much better instrument but a different technique. Beethoven's early piano sonatas with their requirements of fortissimo as well as pianissimo playing were to do much to stimulate piano-makers into building heavier and more powerful instruments with faster actions and pedals. In the early part of the nineteenth century it was said that Beethoven had given the piano its 'soul'. If that meant anything, it was an indication that the instrument was evolving rapidly to meet the demands of much more expressive music that needed to be audible in halls larger than salons. But even in the 1790s it was noted that Beethoven's playing of his slow movements would often move his aristocratic listeners to tears. No other pianist of his day managed that.

Beethoven's comparative penury in those early days in Vienna also threw him into less grand company, and there is abundant evidence that he fell in with people of his own age who shared revolutionary and radical beliefs. No doubt they endorsed Robespierre's stirring motto of *Liberté, Égalité, Fraternité*. The storming of the Bastille had occurred when Beethoven was eighteen and a half, and the extent to which he as a youth was affected by the French Revolution has been much debated. It is probably less significant than the question of how much of his adolescent idealism later persisted in the adult composer, what shape it took, and the degree to which it influenced the 'Eroica' Symphony. French twentieth-century

Johann Georg Albrechtsberger (1736–1809) was the Kapellmeister of St Stephen's Cathedral who inherited Beethoven as a pupil from Haydn. Albrechtsberger gave Beethoven fugue and counterpoint lessons thrice weekly for over a year, later commenting on his pupil's stubbornness while Beethoven derided his teacher's compositions as 'musical skeletons'. The portrait, dating from around 1800, is anonymous.

biographers' opinions usually fell somewhere on the spectrum between that of the composer Vincent d'Indy, who implausibly claimed that Beethoven was entirely uninfluenced by the French Revolution and its progressive ideas (an impossibility, given his age and background), and the writer Romain Rolland, who hailed him as a true 'Son of the French Revolution'.[2]

Almost as soon as he had arrived in Vienna Beethoven joined in a public subscription for a book of Jacobin verse by one Eulogius Schneider ('the Marat of Strasbourg'), whom Beethoven had known back in Bonn when Schneider was teaching Greek literature at the university. The storming of the Bastille had clearly galvanized Schneider's muse, and one of his poems began 'Oh dear Guillotine! How welcome thou art!' which nicely set the volume's general tone.

Like Prague, Vienna of the day was a magnet for students and artists of all kinds living bohemian lives of semi-penury as well as genuine Bohemians from what is today's Czech Republic, many of whom were outstanding musicians. In fact, young hotheads needed to watch their step. The recent developments in France were sending shivers of alarm through Europe's royal families. No matter how enlightened any despot fancied himself to be, a despot he remained. Within days of the fall of the Bastille the Austrian emperor Joseph II reversed many of the liberal social policies he had previously endorsed. A certain Count Pergen, a zealous reactionary, was appointed minister of police to take over the management of censorship from Mozart's old patron and lodge brother, Baron Gottfried van Swieten.[3] Within a short time newspapers were censored, suspected radicals arrested and imprisoned without trial, and even the Freemasons were menaced. When Joseph died in 1790 his brother and successor Leopold II maintained the police state Joseph had inaugurated in such panic. When Leopold himself died after a reign of barely two years, he was succeeded by his son, Francis II, who likewise had no intention of dismantling the state security apparatus. By then the Austrians had mostly forgiven Joseph his reformist excesses and looked back to his reign with affection.

The power and reach of the secret police in Austria's unwieldy empire were considerable, and even small provincial cities such as Salzburg had long been full of spies. The clandestine reading of mail was common if correspondents were suspected of even mildly subversive views. Like many others, Mozart and his father had occasionally used a private code in their letters when mentioning politically sensitive matters. Things were even worse in Vienna, despite the capital's apparent preoccupation with music-making and pleasure-seeking. The young Beethoven rapidly acquired a reputation for political intransigence and unconventional religious views that was to last the remaining thirty-odd years of his life. In a diary entry in 1793 he wrote, 'Do as much good as you can – love freedom above everything. Never deny the truth, not even to the throne.' For the rest of his life he showed no reluctance whatever in loudly airing what he thought of as the truth with splendid impartiality, whether speaking to the throne, to a cardinal or to a stranger in a pub. He would share his scathing attacks on politicians and the aristocracy with anyone who would listen. Yet his was more the outspokenness of an opinionated egotist than of a revolutionary, and it was often aided by drink, a violent temper if thwarted and an increasing refusal to observe dress codes and conventions. This was especially apparent when dealing with the aristocracy, whom he treated familiarly as equals when, indeed, he deigned to recognize them at all.

His impatience with Vienna for not at once offering him a suitable paid post merely increased his antipathy towards its citizens in general. It would have depressed him immeasurably had he known he was in fact destined to live there for the remainder of his life, restlessly changing his lodgings and escaping to the surrounding countryside whenever he could.

He was essentially a small-town boy who never really felt at home in the big city. He soon gave up on the Austrians' revolutionary potential and had harsh things to say about them, both in conversation and in letters. 'So long as your Austrian gets his brown beer and sausages he's not about to join a revolution', he wrote to a friend back in Bonn, the publisher Nikolaus Simrock, on 2 August 1794. 'Double-damned mangy, Viennese trash!'[4] he would growl. Or if referring to an individual, 'Scruffy scoundrel! Stingy riff-raff!'[5] Vienna was a city of two hundred thousand people, and in his opinion most of them were either aristocratic fops and wastrels or scum from all corners of the Habsburg Empire, the whole lot being dedicated to carnal pleasures of the lowest and most frivolous kind. By comparison Bonn (he must have told himself and others countless times) was not at all like that, being a quiet and self-contained Rhenish town of fewer than twenty thousand inhabitants with a musically literate Elector, an excellent court orchestra and people who knew how to behave – excluding, regrettably, his own late father (whose name he would never mention). For all that he himself was fated to die of drink-induced liver failure, Beethoven retained some distinctly provincial, even Puritan, attitudes, especially on sexual matters.

From quite early on the Vienna police must have opened a file on this difficult foreigner given to frequent anti-clerical pronouncements and loud saloon-bar dissections of eminent public figures. Since he habitually referred to priests by the derogatory term *Pfaffen* and his letters were full of profanities, it was put about by his enemies that he was an out-and-out atheist, although there would come a day when 'pantheist' would be a more accurate description. As for his politics, Beethoven's first biographer Anton Schindler[6] was probably accurate when he observed that in his leanings Beethoven was a Republican. The extraordinary Albanian polymath and scholar Fan S. Noli (1882–1965) was even more specific:

All the slogans of the French Revolution can be found in Beethoven's writings and, sometimes, in places where we hardly expect them, in business letters and love letters. And it must be borne in mind that all those slogans were anathema to the old regime of Vienna, which considered them dangerous to the state and forbade their use to its citizens.[7]

Yet despite the perils Beethoven thrived, increasingly successful as both performer and composer, presumably well enough protected by his aristocratic mentors. Then in February 1798 the French Directorate sent General Jean Bernadotte to Vienna as its ambassador. He was young, handsome, dashing and had distinguished himself as Napoleon's aide-de-camp in his Italian campaign. Viennese ladies fell for him in heaps; the city authorities much less so. Ambassador he might have been; diplomat he was not. Apart from sporting the French tricolour in his hat and addressing everybody impartially as 'citizen', he and his retinue would hiss in the theatre when anyone cried, 'Long live Emperor Francis!'[8] Bernadotte was musical and brought with him France's foremost violinist, Rodolphe

Kreutzer. Prince Lichnowsky, by this time one of Beethoven's several noble patrons, introduced Beethoven to Bernadotte and Kreutzer. By all accounts the feisty composer and the two Frenchmen hit it off. Bernadotte had brought with him a collection of revolutionary music from Paris by composers such as Méhul, Le Sueur, Gossec, Catel and Kreutzer himself, which Beethoven studied eagerly.

Some of this music would already have been familiar to him from his days in the court orchestra in Bonn, but there was much that was new. This was music for open-air festivities and official celebrations, often martial. The essence of the style was that it should be stirring, the supreme example being Rouget de Lisle's magnificent setting of 'La Marseillaise', written in Strasbourg in 1792 just after France had declared war on Austria. Above all, it was designed to be 'people's music'; anything too 'learned', such as counterpoint, had been purged from it. Rather it emphasized memorable, singable tunes that crowds could easily pick up, often with a degree of quasi-Masonic solemnity.[9] (Something of the same prescription would be used after 1860 for the Church of England's *Hymns Ancient and Modern* with their narrow vocal range and simple Mendelssohnian harmonies.) It might not be too fanciful to see the tune Beethoven used in 1823 to set Schiller's 'Ode to Joy' for the Ninth Symphony as owing something to this French revolutionary music.

General Bernadotte's appointment was destined to last fewer than three months. In April he was recalled, having gone too far in his revolutionary fervour by flying the French tricolour from his hotel, which incited a stone-throwing mob of patriotic Viennese to attack the building. This in turn led to Bernadotte making bombastic flourishes with his sword and noisily vowing to slay 'members of the rabble' (formerly 'citizens'). He had to be saved by a detachment of the emperor's cavalry as the crowd set fire to the French flag.

In November 1799 Napoleon led a coup against the increasingly corrupt and inefficient post-revolutionary Directorate and replaced it with the Consulate, in true Roman style appointing himself First Consul. The Battle of Marengo in 1800 was his decisive victory over the Habsburg `empire, driving the Austrians out of Italy and greatly reinforcing his own pre-eminent position. In the Vienna of 1800 it would have been easy for Beethoven, in common with many thoughtful and politically aware people, to foresee that within a very few years the whole of central Europe might well come under French administration, and who knew for how long? Certainly Napoleon seemed militarily unstoppable.

To this uncertain political future could be added Beethoven's worry at his failure so far to find a secure paid position in Vienna. True, he had acquired a stable of aristocratic patrons who between them were generously supportive, even in the face of his occasional bouts of boorishness: a tribute to their musical discernment. They included Prince Joseph Lobkowitz, Baron Gottfried van Swieten, Prince Karl Lichnowsky and Count Andreas Razumovsky. These gentlemen are posthumously due history's gratitude in that they were perceptive enough to humour, indulge and support Beethoven financially with commissions despite his contempt for their social position and their city. But like most artists throughout the ages (and everybody else) what Beethoven really wanted was the financial security of a regular income. He already entertained a socialist – or possibly schoolboy – fantasy of the ideal artist's life, when there would exist a single ministry of art for the entire world. The artist would merely hand in his work in exchange for the money he needed.[10] Such a utopian dream hardly accorded with the system of patronage that still obtained in the city where the immigrant Beethoven earned his living.

In the first two or three years of the new century he began quietly planning a move to Paris. His idea was that not only would the French capital be an improvement on Vienna but to take up residence there might also be a canny career move. Apart from anything else Beethoven was ambitious to see his compositions published abroad. By now he had acquired a young student and admirer, Ferdinand Ries, who in exchange for lessons acted as an informal agent, one of whose duties was to make contact with foreign publishers. On 6 August 1803 Ries wrote to the publisher Simrock in Bonn, saying Beethoven would be staying in Vienna for only another eighteen months, being determined to move to Paris. Ries was depressed about this plan and admitted he had jokingly dropped broad hints to Beethoven that he hoped he could go

with him as the composer's 'student and financial manager'. It is safe to assume Beethoven had been mulling over this radical move for some time before telling Ries.

In view of events that suggested French influence in Europe could only increase in the foreseeable future, Beethoven evidently calculated that it would make sense to take advantage of Paris as the likely future centre of European culture. After all, his music was already known to Parisian music-lovers, and printed editions were available in music shops there. His First Symphony had been performed there and probably the Second as well. Both had been found agreeable and interestingly different without being too aggressively 'modern'. However, Beethoven was probably over-estimating French receptivity to his orchestral music, since the 'Eroica' was not to be performed in Paris until 1825, some twenty-two years after it was composed, when it was compared to the two earlier symphonies and not to its advantage.

For some years now Beethoven had evidently been thinking seriously about writing something inspired by – if not actually a tribute to – Napoleon. In 1802 he had begun sketches for a symphony but had laid them aside in order to finish other work. By early 1803 Beethoven had decided to take two big new works with him to France to act as calling cards: an opera and a symphony. He was already at work on the opera; the symphony would be the 'Eroica'. By the end of that summer the 'Eroica' was finished and in another letter to

Prince Karl Lichnowsky by an unknown artist. The Prince was Vienna's leading musical patron. He shared the same Masonic lodge as Mozart and had been one of his pupils. He befriended the young Beethoven and helped arrange his studies with Haydn and Albrechtsberger. In 1806 Lichnowsky and Beethoven had a serious falling-out and were never wholly reconciled before the Prince's death in 1814.

Simrock on 22 October Ries wrote that Beethoven had recently played it through on the piano to him and very much wanted to dedicate it to Bonaparte. Since then he had turned his attention to other things, including the opera, which, Ries said, was a setting in German of the French librettist Jean-Nicolas Bouilly's *Léonore, ou l'amour conjugale*: a 'rescue opera' whose plot had already been used by other composers.

The 'rescue opera' was a genre pioneered by Cherubini's *Lodoïska*, which had been first performed to wild acclaim in Paris back in July 1791. This type of story, full of evil tyrants holding in servitude and chains innocents who were eventually freed in a grand climax, had become very popular in revolutionary France, combining as it did patriotism, idealism and an urge to sweep away the old regime. The idea of the triumph of freedom and justice undoubtedly appealed to Beethoven, who calculated that the genre's popularity would ensure his own opera's success. After all, Bouilly had also written the libretto of Cherubini's *Les Deux Journées*, which had taken Vienna by storm a couple of years earlier. Ries reckoned his teacher would probably need eighteen months to finish the opera and so was hopeful of being able to accompany Beethoven to Paris late the following year or in early 1805. In fact the opera (initially called *Léonore* but soon renamed *Fidelio*) was finished by early 1804, having given Beethoven a good deal of trouble, and had already been bought by the Theater an der Wien. By this time the opera's theme was interpreted as less subversive of the Habsburg

Empire than supportive of pan-Germanism faced with the Napoleonic threat.

Considering that Beethoven had considered defecting to Paris even before composing the 'Eroica' in the summer of 1803 and given also his known earlier republican sympathies with revolutionary France and its figurehead, Napoleon Bonaparte, how is one to assess the French influence on the symphony? There is reason to suspect Beethoven had considerably revised the revolutionary enthusiasms he had nurtured in his twenties, and he had probably already put his plans to move to Paris on hold on account of musical commitments in Vienna and the now serious deafness that was causing him much misery. At any rate it was surely significant that a full year earlier in the spring of 1802 he had written a decisive letter to one of his publishers, the composer Franz Anton Hoffmeister, who had recently moved to Vienna and had already published the '*Pathétique*' Piano Sonata.

Evidently Hoffmeister and others had suggested he wrote some kind of revolutionary or Bonapartist sonata. Only the year before, Austria's Francis II, who was also the Holy Roman Emperor, had signed the Treaty of Lunéville with France following the defeat at Marengo, since when the Austrian Empire had been obliged to make a series of humiliating territorial concessions. Hoffmeister's suggestion was presumably intended to cash in on the Austrians' abiding – if nervous – interest in Napoleon's future intentions. Beethoven was having none of it.

Vienna, 8 April 1802
May the devil ride the whole lot of you, gentlemen — what, suggest I
should write a sonata of that sort? At the time of the revolutionary fever
— well, then it might have been worth a thought. But now that everything
is trying to get back into the old rut and Bonaparte has made his
concordat with the Pope — a sonata of that sort. . . ? at the beginning
of this new Christian era? Ha ha! Count me out, for nothing will come
of it.

The satirical religious reference was to the Concordat Napoleon had agreed with the Pope, Pius VII, in July 1801, which undertook to reverse the French revolutionary decree that Church and State should be separate entities. Although by 1809 Beethoven had long since abandoned his plans to go abroad, Jérôme Bonaparte, Napoleon's brother, was to offer Beethoven the job of Kapellmeister in Westphalia. Beethoven didn't consider this seriously for a moment, but he did use the offer craftily to strengthen his bid for an annuity when dealing with his patrons. He finally got what he wanted from Archduke Rudolph, Prince Lobkowitz and Prince Kinsky when they offered him an annuity for life provided he promised to stay in Vienna. He promised; and by then thankfully.

But back in April 1802 and in the light of his early sketches for a Bonaparte symphony only a couple of months later, it seems his intentions were musically grander as well as less focused on the immediate political situation. It is likely that the figure of 'Bonaparte', as processed by Beethoven's imagination, was based on the man he had once seen as spreading the

Prince Franz Joseph Lobkowitz, one of three noble patrons who had agreed to keep Beethoven financially afloat by paying him a stipend. By 1810, as a result of the Napoleonic war, inflation in Austria had sent the cost of living up so much that Lobkowitz had long defaulted on his payments to Beethoven and was himself virtually bankrupt. The portrait is an anonymous copy in oils of an original painting by August Friedrich Oelenhainz.

Napoleon Bonaparte in his study at the Tuileries in 1812 by Jacques-Louis David. According to the painter this portrait was designed to show the Emperor slightly dishevelled after a sleepless night spent drafting the Code Napoléon (visible on the desk). The guttering candle and the clock show the hour to be that of dawn, the sword on the chair evidences his military prowess.

egalitarian and secular ideal of the French Revolution throughout Europe and even the world. The Corsican who now did deals with the Vatican to reinstate the Church's stifling hegemony was no longer Beethoven's Bonaparte. The French army had long been in possession of his beloved birthplace, Bonn, together with the previously German left bank of the Rhine, and was threatening Vienna and the Habsburg Empire. So whose side was he on now? Beethoven was by no means alone in facing this quandary: it was shared by half Europe's intellectuals. (The subject will be explored in Chapter 7, which deals with the question of the dedication of the 'Eroica'.) And any theory of Napoleon's exact significance to Beethoven at the time he was writing his ground-breaking symphony is further muddied by the conflation in his mind of the French conqueror with another hero, this one mythical: Prometheus.

4

PROMETHEUS

In Greek mythology Prometheus was a divine helper of mankind, albeit an ambivalent one. Having stolen fire from Zeus, the supreme deity, he gave it to the human race. Beware of Greeks bearing gifts (as Virgil wisely warned), for fire was to prove a mixed blessing. In obvious respects it was a boon, providing light and heat; but in time it would lead to destructive technologies that would enslave mankind. Zeus, furious at the theft, exacted a twofold punishment. He created Pandora, the first woman, to spread misfortune among the human race, a task she ably achieved with her allegorical box (actually a jar) of assorted evils. He then had Prometheus bound to a stake on Mount Kaukasos where an eagle regularly flew in to snack on his liver, which regenerated itself between the bird's agonizing visits.

It is not hard to see why this myth might have had powerful private significance for Beethoven. From at least 1800 he had been forced to confront his increasing deafness as a permanent condition that would now never be reversed. He had done his best to maintain a brave optimism that this or that doctor prescribing this or that treatment might miraculously effect a cure. But in his heart he must have known it was of no avail and that he must resign himself to a future in which he could no longer earn his living as a lionized performer and instead subsist only on what he could earn from his compositions. Like Prometheus's liver, his deafness seemed self-perpetuating and destined to cause him constant anguish.

When asked in 1800 to write the orchestral music for a ballet called *The Creatures of Prometheus* he presumably welcomed it as just another paid commission, albeit an important one, since it was for Vienna's Burgtheater and was to be designed by the famous ballet-master Salvatore Viganò. But as he worked on the lengthy score (a good hour's worth of music) the Promethean myth of the eternally suffering hero must have suggested striking parallels with his own predicament and even with his idealized but inconsistent identification with Napoleon Bonaparte. Was Napoleon not a bringer of freedom's fire, a great uplifted torch, as a gift to mankind? And was this freedom not being stolen from the formerly godlike figures of Europe's reigning monarchs and popes? True, he would doubtless pay for it later: in Greek mythology hubris was always punished. But the gift had been given. The secret of mankind's freedom was out and surely could never now be recaptured.

And then – a step further – why might Beethoven not view himself as a spiritual henchman of Bonaparte, his music bringing fire and light and showing that the brotherhood of man would prevail? Chained to the rock of his private fate he might be constantly tormented, but like Prometheus himself he had unconquerable will. That at least endured: Beethoven never lost his belief in the ultimate triumph of his music and its message to all humanity.

It inevitably sounds fanciful and novelistic to ascribe such detailed intentions to anyone, let alone to a genius working in an abstract art at a time of great political unrest well over two centuries ago. And yet the evidence is strong that Beethoven's muse, at least, perceived such parallels. It is unfortunate that the original choreography for Viganò's Prometheus ballet has not survived, so the exact onstage context of each of the sixteen numbers remains guesswork. What is not guesswork is the significance of the ballet score to the 'Eroica' Symphony that was beginning to occupy another part of Beethoven's brain. There are significant parallels between the works. The adventurous sonorities and effects of the fullest orchestra he had so far used became those of the 'Eroica': the ballet's use of three horns, for example, which were to reappear so memorably in the trio of the symphony's *Scherzo*; the use of syncopation; the influence of his French contemporaries in the martial passages with their drums and trumpets.

However, despite – or maybe because of – Beethoven's large and complex score, the ballet *Die Geschöpfe des Prometheus* was not a great success. A certain J. C. Rosenbaum went to a rehearsal and later wrote, 'The ballet was not at all well received, the music little better. . . At the end the ballet was more hissed down than applauded.'[1] By then Haydn was back from his second visit to England. Since the huge success of his 1798 oratorio *The Creation* (*Die Schöpfung*) the celebrated composer was at the height of his fame, often referred to affectionately as 'Papa' Haydn. He went along to a performance of the ballet, probably curious to see what his brilliant but difficult pupil had been doing while he had been away. The next day

OVERLEAF
Heiligenstadt village at around the time of Beethoven's residence in the early 1800s. His doctors recommended rural tranquillity to save what was left of his hearing, and the bucolic scene with the view across the Danube to the foothills of the Carpathians on the horizon must have afforded him solace.

BMd 1

Gli Uomini di Prometeo

BALLO

per il Clavicembalo o Piano-Forte

Composto, e dedicato

à Sua Altezza la Signora Principessa

LICHNOWSKY nata CONTESSA THUNN

da

Luiggi van Beethoven

Opera 24

In Vienna presso Artaria e Comp.

872

Beethoven ran into his former teacher in the street. According to Robbins Landon, Haydn stopped him and said:

"'Now, yesterday I heard your ballet and it pleased me very much.' Beethoven thereupon answered, 'Oh, my dear Papa, you are very kind, but it is very far from being a "Creation".' Haydn, surprised and almost offended by this answer, said after a short silence, 'That is true, it is not yet a "Creation" and I very much doubt whether it will ever succeed in being one.' Whereupon each of them, somewhat dumbfounded, took leave of the other. The play on words, 'Geschöpfe' and 'Schöpfung', which Beethoven used to taunt his former teacher, does not come off in English; but even without it the insult must have appalled the courteous Haydn. Relations between the two men were now deteriorating to the point of no return, and from the documentary evidence at our disposal it is clearly Beethoven who wished to disassociate himself from Haydn, not vice versa." [2]

From Landon's account it is difficult to see what was offensive in what Beethoven said. The great Haydn scholar's gloss notwithstanding, it must be remembered that Beethoven had a lifelong habit of crude and ill-judged puns. By a long way this was neither the first nor last occasion that his hit-or-miss wordplay gave unintended offence to someone. Yet no matter what jealousy he might still have nurtured for his laurelled ex-teacher's international success, it seems most unlikely that Beethoven's clumsy attempt at wit was a deliberate 'taunt' and, given that Haydn was well aware of the 'Grand Mogul's' social awkwardness, it seems equally improbable that he would have taken offence.

The title page of the 1801 piano version of Beethoven's score for the ballet *The Creatures of Prometheus* of the previous year, with the composer's own scribbled instructions. The ballet itself was not a success although Beethoven's orchestral score pointed clearly towards the Eroica, above all in the little dance number that was to become the theme of the Symphony's finale.

It is a great pity that although the ballet's overture is quite often played, the rest of the music remains little known to the majority of concertgoers even though they would instantly recognize the last tune in the finale. Beethoven reused the one he had just written for the seventh of a set of twelve little contre-dances (WoO14), which in turn might have had its roots in his early Bonn piano quartets.* The first violins have the tune:

In the ballet's finale Beethoven worked this simple tune up with contrasting sections, almost as if it were an orchestrated version of one of his bagatelles for piano. It must have had a particular significance for him because once the ballet was out of the way he went straight on to use it yet again, this time for a set of fifteen variations and a fugue for piano. At one level

---

* See Chapter 2, p. 31.

this was a showpiece for Beethoven himself as a virtuoso performer since it is a compendium of pianistic tricks that include hand-crossing, rapid skips and glittering passagework. In this instance the tune, as it first appears, is in the top line:

At another level these taxing variations clearly functioned as a kind of trial run for the 'Eroica' Symphony's *Finale*, which is based on the same tune used yet again in the same rhythm and key and treated with even greater inventiveness, fugue and all. In fact, the form in both cases is unique in musical history. Never before or since had a set of piano variations started not with the main tune but with a bald, 16-bar statement of its bass line alone:

Thereafter this bare outline gathers accompanying voices until the main theme is finally stated. The symphony's *Finale* begins in the same way, only this time it takes 67 bars until the 'Prometheus' tune is heard in full. So famous did this theme become as the symphony's *Finale* that the earlier piano work is known today as the *Eroica Variations*, Op. 35, rather than the 'Prometheus Variations'. The tune's musical significance is that it perfectly lends itself to almost limitless development and elaboration. Certainly in its earliest version as a little dance tune it gave no hint of the potential for its own apotheosis as a grand symphonic finale.

Unlike the ballet, the piano variations were very well received, and so they should have been given their remarkable originality. Variation 10 in particular, with its impressionistic fragmentation of the theme and its outrageous tonal surprises, inhabits a world akin to that of the *Diabelli Variations*, Op. 120, of some twenty years later. A critic in the 22 February 1804 issue of the respected Leipzig weekly, *Allgemeine musikalische Zeitung*, was to write a lengthy and admiring review of Op. 35:

*Inexhaustible imagination, original humour and deep, intimate, even
passionate feeling are the particular features that give rise to the ingenious
character that distinguishes nearly all Herr van Beethoven's works. This
earns him one of the highest places among first-rate instrumental
composers. His latest works in particular show the care he takes to
maintain a chosen character and to combine the greatest freedom with
purity of phrasing and contrapuntal elegance. All this composer's
peculiarities just cited can be found to a marked degree in this work. Even
its overall form, which deviates so far from what is customary, bears
witness to unmistakable genius.[3]*

The 'deviation', of course, was the unheard-of idea of starting
a set of variations without immediately stating the theme to be
varied. Or, rather, without any music critic being quite sure if
that really was what Beethoven had done. The absurdly naked
bass line that gradually gathers harmonic garments before at
last appearing fully clothed as the 'Prometheus' tune: might
that not actually *be* the main theme? To this day, nobody can
say for certain.

   Where the Prometheus myth itself was concerned,
Beethoven's classically educated contemporaries would have
spotted the parallels easily enough when eventually they heard
the symphony a few years later. Many then no doubt recalled
seeing the ballet and recognized its symbolic elements in the
symphony's four movements that one by one outlined the
sequence of struggle, death, rebirth and apotheosis. As for
the theme's inner significance to its composer, it is quite
difficult for us today *not* to see this notion of Promethean

Andante con moto

creativity and punishment as a multiple metaphor. For him the political struggle of the times was intimately tied in with his shifting opinion of Napoleon Bonaparte and France in general. At a private level there was above all his penitential battle with deafness. There would also have been associations with his rescue opera *Fidelio*, which at the time was constantly and naggingly on his mind. A prisoner being brought up from a Stygian dungeon into bright sunlight was a perfect Promethean motif. And at an obscurer level still there was his struggle as a composer to forge a new music in the teeth of the old, not to mention finally being able to step out of 'Papa' Haydn's shadow.

The Op. 35 *Eroica Variations* were written at perhaps the most despairing point of Beethoven's life, and it is extraordinary that their creative energy and even humour betray no hint of this. Beethoven's new physician, Dr Johann Schmidt, had urged the composer to spare his hearing the din of the big city and retreat to the countryside. So in the summer of 1802 Beethoven took up residence in Heiligenstadt: in those days a pretty hamlet just to the west of Vienna with vistas across the Danube to the Carpathians on the horizon. The rooms he took in a farmhouse had uninterrupted views up a secluded valley behind the house: in fact the very valley he was later to walk while composing the 'Pastoral' Symphony. Yet despite the peacefulness of his surroundings, his life's major crisis was steadily overwhelming him even as he wrote the piano variations. Matters came to a head in early October when he

The autograph of the *Eroica Variations* for piano, Op. 35 (1802). Since it was inherited from the ballet of two years earlier the theme of the variations ought really to be called the Prometheus Theme; but Beethoven's use of it yet again in the following year for the *Eroica* Symphony's finale has made the later association indelible. This page of the finale shows the calm restatement of the theme immediately following the athletic fugue.

scrawled the despairing document known today as the Heiligenstadt Testament. In the guise of a last will and testament citing his two brothers as joint heirs, it is a cry from the heart: by turns self-pitying, resigned and histrionic. Even today it is impossible to read it without being moved by Beethoven's depression as he apologizes for having appeared to his family and friends as difficult, morose and misanthropic while all the time not daring to divulge the reason, his darkest secret: that he was going deaf.

Beethoven had evidently become aware of a problem with his hearing in around 1796 when he was still only twenty-five and at the peak of his career as a pianist. He waited a further four years before admitting it for the first time in a touching and intimate letter dated 1 June 1800 to his close Viennese friend Carl Amenda. After a further two years when the deafness had inexorably progressed, he poured his heart out in the Heiligenstadt Testament addressed to his younger brothers. In it Beethoven described himself as still only twenty-eight whereas in fact he was nearly thirty-two. (He was always confused about his birth date because his father Johann used randomly to knock years off his age as a boy to make him appear a more marketable 'Wunderkind'). It is a pitiful confession, as though of a crime. 'For me there can be no relaxation in human company, decent conversation, mutual exchanges. I can talk to people only when it is absolutely necessary. I must live like an exile', he wrote. 'If I come near people a hot terror seizes me, a dread of putting myself in danger that they will detect my condition.' And on and on in the same vein, erratic punctuation betraying his lack of elementary schooling. It is dated 'Heiglnstadt [*sic*] October 6 1802'. Four days later he added an even more heartbroken codicil:

Heiglnstadt October 10 1802. So I take leave of you – and sadly, for the blessed hope I brought here that I might at least be partly cured must now be utterly abandoned. It has withered like the falling leaves of autumn. I go away again almost as I came. Even the high courage that often inspired me in the beautiful days of summer has vanished. Oh Providence! Just give me one day of pure joy: it is so long since I heard the inner echo of real happiness. Oh immortal spirit! When, oh when can I once again feel it in the temple of nature and mankind? Never? No – oh, that would be too cruel.

Whatever else, this is not the fervent prayer of an orthodox Catholic. There are no appeals to the Virgin or the saints, and even God is de-Christianized as Providence. Together with the use of the word 'temple' the tone harks back to the usage of his old teacher Christian Neefe and his Masonic friends in the Bonn of his adolescence. The Heiligenstadt Testament reads almost like a suicide note – it was, after all, his will – except of course that Beethoven did not kill himself despite admitting 'only a little more and I would have put an end to my life, it was only art that held me back. Ah! it seemed impossible to leave the world until I had produced everything I felt capable of, and so I carried on my miserable existence …' This is the record of someone confronting the lowest point of his life, realizing

he would not be cured, that his natural social ineptness was fatally worsened by being deaf, that he was doomed always to be misunderstood and never to acquire a partner, that he truly was alone. One wonders if years later when he was writing the choral finale of the Ninth Symphony it would seem painfully ironic as he set the lines in Schiller's 'Ode' that run:

Whoever has won a beloved wife,
Let him add to the jubilation! …
And he who never achieved marriage,
Let him slink away in tears!

But by then he must have been long resigned to his fate. Despite an earlier succession of quite unrealistic romantic hopes, he had always been doomed to die a bachelor.

The Heiligenstadt Testament is undoubtedly a tragic document. Yet even so, it is hard for modern readers to know why Beethoven should have experienced his deafness as quite such a profound source of shame. Maybe it was more a shrinking from the consequences: the irony of a musician losing his most precious asset; the end of his livelihood of public performing; foreseeing the magnanimous pity of bitter rivals and inferiors who would now eagerly reclaim the limelight he had to leave. Yet the tone of this 'confession' is similar to that of someone in a twentieth-century suicide note describing a sexuality that he felt had made him a social outcast ('a dread of putting myself in danger that they will detect my condition'). One might have imagined that in Beethoven's day of dubious medical recourse – the quack doctors, epidemic

The first page of the Heiligenstadt Testament. Headed 'For my brothers Carl and   Beethoven', it is an impassioned document somewhere between a Will and a confession. For an unknown reason Beethoven had a lifelong reluctance to name his youngest brother, Nikolaus Johann, hence the blank before the family name. Despite the document's heading it often seems as though Beethoven is addressing humanity at large as much as his own kith and kin.

diseases, untreatable disabilities and early deaths – his deafness was more likely to have attracted matter-of-factness and sympathy. After all, he must have known for some time that his playing was becoming increasingly inaccurate. He would have glimpsed occasional winces in faces that once were rapt and tearful. But his life furnishes ample evidence of how bad he was at judging people's reactions, having very little under-standing of either himself or of others. It was not just his puns he misjudged: he had simply never acquired many of the basics of ordinary human relations. Beethoven was hopelessly ill equipped to deal with his own overwhelming genius, and his deafness only threw it and him into increasing proximity.

Yet in some way the Heiligenstadt crisis must have been cathartic because his truly Promethean creativity never flagged. While working on the piano variations in that summer of 1802 he had also been playing around with ideas for a grand new symphony. Beethoven's copious sketches for what was to become the 'Eroica' provide a fascinating insight into what one might call his purposeful gropings towards its final version. In Heiligenstadt he made sketches for the first three movements but seemed not to bother with the finale, presumably since he must already have decided on a set of orchestral variations and fugue on the same 'Prometheus' theme, and its outlines were probably clear enough in his mind not to need roughing out at this stage. Obviously its key of E flat major would determine that of the symphony as a whole. As it turned out, he never used these initial drafts. They were part of the laborious craft by which he slowly constructed all his masterpieces as one by one the ideas became clearer to him. After that autumn in Heiligenstadt he shelved the work while keeping it very much alive at the back of his mind.

The best part of a year then went by while he worked at a steady pace on commissions, finishing the Second Symphony, the three violin sonatas, Op. 30, the three piano sonatas, Op. 31, an unsuccessful oratorio *Christus am Oelberge* ('Christ on the Mount of Olives') and much else besides. Then in the early summer of 1803, in response to his usual urge to get out of Vienna's dust and noise into the countryside, he again rented rooms, this time in Oberdöbling, not far from Heiligenstadt. Armed with his own heroic acceptance of his fate and a new sketchbook he settled down to serious work on the symphony. In the interim he must have done a good deal of thinking and now had a much clearer idea of where the piece was going. At some point the project had jelled around a 'programme' he would probably have been unable to describe schematically, but which had evidently taken overall shape in his mind as partly occupying the portentous spaces defined by 'Bonaparte' and 'heroism' and partly reflecting his own renewed dedication to his exacting muse.

5

CONSTRUCTING
A SYMPHONY

How far should one go in presuming to link biographical detail with an artwork? There has long been a tendency among certain biographers, especially modern ones, to try to 'get inside' Beethoven's mind during the creative process. The spur to this has usually been the archive of sketches and other documents he carefully hoarded. Older composers such as Haydn, Mozart and above all Bach have been largely spared the more graphic of such attempts, because they left comparatively few – if any – such pointers as to how a particular work was conceived, as opposed to noting who had commissioned it. A fascination with people's emotional states was very much a Romantic phenomenon and one perfectly exemplified by Beethoven's contemporary, the composer–writer E. T. A. Hoffmann, who was to write so passionately about Beethoven and most famously about the Fifth Symphony. This is how Hoffmann began his rhapsody about 'a work that is splendid beyond all measure':

How irresistibly does this wonderful composition transport the listener through ever growing climaxes into the spiritual realm of the infinite. . . The character of apprehensive, restless longing contained in this movement is made even plainer by the melodious subsidiary theme. The breast that is oppressed and alarmed by intimations of things monstrous, destructive, and threatening wheezes for air with wrenching gasps.[1]

The oppressed breast and wrenching gasps are suggestive of Henry Fuseli's painting *The Nightmare* (1782) and the whole consumptive world of the emerging Romantic period. Who knows if it bore even the remotest connection to Beethoven's creative process? This particular way of writing about music was the progenitor of some of the worst purple passages in the history of Western literature, many of them perpetrated about the same symphony. Perhaps the most notorious example is that in Chapter 5 of E. M. Forster's novel *Howards End*, describing a performance in the Queen's Hall, London. Forster's editorializing begins with the bland and unverifiable assertion, 'It will be generally admitted that Beethoven's Fifth Symphony is the most sublime noise that has ever penetrated into the ear of man.' His ensuing description tells us nothing whatever about the music and everything about the musically illiterate English middle-classes of the Bloomsbury period. We begin at the end of the slow movement:

Here Beethoven, after humming and hawing with great sweetness, said 'Heigho', and the Andante came to an end. . . Helen said to her aunt: 'Now comes the wonderful movement: first of all the goblins, and then a trio of elephants dancing. . . Look out for the part where you think you have done with the goblins and they come back,' breathed Helen, as the music started with a goblin walking quietly over the universe, from end to end. Others followed him. They were not aggressive creatures; it was that that made them so terrible to Helen. They merely observed in passing that there was no such thing as splendour or heroism in the world. After the interlude of elephants dancing, they returned and made the observation for the second time. Helen could not contradict them, for, once at all events, she had felt the same, and had seen the reliable walls of youth collapse. Panic and emptiness! Panic and emptiness! The goblins were right. Her brother raised his finger; it was the transitional passage on the drum. For, as if things were going too far, Beethoven took hold of the goblins and made them do what he wanted. He appeared in person. He gave them a little push, and they began to walk in a major key instead of in a minor, and then — he blew with his mouth and they were scattered! Gusts of splendour, gods and demigods contending with vast swords, colour and fragrance broadcast on the field of battle, magnificent victory, magnificent death! Oh, it all burst before the girl, and she even stretched out her gloved hands as if it was tangible. Any fate was titanic; any contest desirable; conqueror and conquered would alike be applauded by the angels of the utmost stars.

Goblins, elephants, demigods, angels. As an accomplished composer himself Hoffmann could surely never have perpetrated this menagerie; but as a Romantic writer raised on the novels of Jean Paul his language was undoubtedly that of the emotions music could evoke and a certain extravagance was always likely. One drawback of this way of writing about music is that it becomes nearly inevitable that such writers confuse their own reactions with the composer's intentions.

There is a case to be made for calling Beethoven the first genius in the modern sense. Previously, an exceptional artist such as Mozart simply *had* genius as a gift from God. It inhabited rather than personified him. But with the writings of Hoffmann the idea of *the* genius took hold: an exceptional artist who by his own efforts rather than supernatural ones transfigured himself into a victorious Olympian, a metamorphosis that requisitioned every aspect of his life and being.

To some extent we still retain this notion. Johann Rochlitz, a tenor singer who knew Beethoven well, once described him

This portrait of Beethoven by
Joseph Mähler, painted around
1804, shows the composer not
long after he had finished the
Eroica. His dapper clothes reflect
his appearance as Vienna's
foremost 'Lion of the keyboard'
even though by now his deafness
has put that career in terminal
decline. Beethoven kept the
painting for the rest of his life,
perhaps as a nostalgic reminder
of his former public glory.

as 'a very able man reared on a desert island and suddenly brought fresh into the world'.[2] And there he is: the Caliban archetype of the modern-style genius untainted by a debased civilization, uncaring of social conventions and even of the law, taking dictation from his inner daemon. A holy man, a sadhu, his body covered in filth and ashes but his mind dwelling among the stars. A certain strand of Beethoven biographies has always helped this image along with imaginative word-portraits of the composer striding tousled about the Austrian landscape, howling snatches of music, stamping his feet to inner rhythms and occasionally stopping to scribble illegible notes on a tattered sheaf of manuscript paper or to shake his fist at the elements as a sort of symphonic King Lear. For all one knows it might have been exactly like that: it remains a harmless fancy. Yet trying to guess the thought processes of creative artists is inevitably presumptuous, no matter what they said about themselves. The same applies to assigning a 'meaning' to a piece of music even if, as with the 'Eroica', the composer assigned it the title 'Bonaparte' from the first and labelled its slow movement 'Funeral March'. Quite enough for speculation; yet nothing like enough for psychoanalytical certainty.

Then there is the problem of the Past, where things were thought and done differently. Was Mozart's late G minor Symphony 'autobiographical'? It is not even clear what this might mean other than in vague terms of the work's 'mood' – and even that is open to radically opposed interpretations.

CONSTRUCTING A SYMPHONY

Today we hear it as redolent of passion and tragedy, whereas Schumann, the arch-romantic and one of the nineteenth century's astutest composer–critics, perceived only a 'Grecian lightness and grace'.

All the same, given what we already know about Beethoven's associations of his Third Symphony with Bonaparte, Prometheus and heroism in general, certain liberties will inevitably have to be taken. Not only did the 'Eroica' break all previous symphonic moulds in its sheer size and complexity, it was also the nineteenth century's first major avant-garde work: one that severely challenged both performers and its audiences. It might be useful to note some of the methods Beethoven used without ascribing too many motives, other than technical, to him.

I ALLEGRO CON BRIO

A resemblance to the theme that opens the 'Eroica' has long been spotted in the tune with which the twelve-year-old Mozart began the overture to his little opera *Bastien et Bastienne* (1768): the notes, rhythm and key are identical to Beethoven's. Scholars have pondered whether Beethoven could have known Mozart's boyhood work, the consensus being that it is possible but unlikely. In any case the notes in question simply make up a chord of E flat major, and firmly establishing the key at the outset was a conventional way of beginning a piece of music. A large part of Beethoven's genius lay in his ability to take the notes of a striking phrase – even just a common chord – and somehow construct an entire movement from them. It was this trick of making distinctive fragments yield up their hidden possibilities that gave rise to the concept of the *Leitmotiv*, which later gained particular currency through Wagner's use of it. As always, Beethoven was ahead of his time.

How he actually began the 'Eroica' immediately confirms how little this symphony was to be beholden to anything that had gone before. The single chord with which he had opened the Op. 35 piano variations has now become two brusque chords for full orchestra that stand like twin great pillars forming the work's portal. This might seem to derive from a similar device Haydn sometimes used in his later works as a 'call to attention', but in Beethoven's hands his grand portal immediately opens onto an E flat tonal landscape that the cellos promptly subvert with a rogue C sharp. It is a completely unexpected move and immediately leaves the hearer slightly off balance:

It is a powerful device (and one that was to be exploited later by Liszt).[*] The exposition of this first movement con-

---

[*]   See Appendix, p. 184.

tinues the unsettled effect by introducing tunes that feel more unfinished than complete in themselves. By the time of the repeat at the double bar-lines (the two great introductory chords are not repeated) it becomes clear on how grand a scale the music is going to be. All these motifs and snatches of tune have to be allowed to expand, link up and make satisfying sense, and from the moment the movement is begun for the second time it is clear this will be a symphony like no other before it. In fact the first movement of the 'Eroica', including repeats, plays longer than many an entire little eighteenth-century symphony.

This is music that needs to be heard rather than analysed, for no matter how familiar it becomes, it miraculously retains a freshness as though one were always hearing it for the first time. This maybe has something to do with its sheer energy. It is an act of self-assertion that at times almost gives the impression that the composer is reaching out of the score to grasp the hearer's lapels. And if this seems too fanciful, the sense of an utterly distinctive musical personality with something new and urgent to say is often overwhelming, not only in the orchestral climaxes but equally in the careful details that defy the listener to ignore them.

There is a famous instance of this at the moment of the recapitulation. After the development section has taken us on an often startling but weirdly logical tour of the landscape in which we have looked at the exposition's fragments from a variety of different angles until they seem to construct an imposing skyline, we are about to return to the home key of E flat major and it is time for the main theme to be restated. It is a normal enough moment in the Classical form so familiar to eighteenth-century listeners, but Beethoven once again wittily destabilizes conventional expectations. The orchestration is reduced to the first and second violins holding a soft tremolo chord in the dominant against which a single horn states the opening theme in the tonic. In other words, even as the violins are playing the notes that most prepare the ear for a return to the symphony's 'home' key of E flat major, the horn appears to jump the gun by being already there:

To the ears of many of Beethoven's listeners what sounded like an awful mistake is actually a moment of pure magic. It was this harmonic clash that led poor Ferdinand Ries, Beethoven's young student and unpaid secretary, to make a gaffe at the rehearsal for the symphony's first semi-public performance by Prince Lobkowitz's private orchestra:

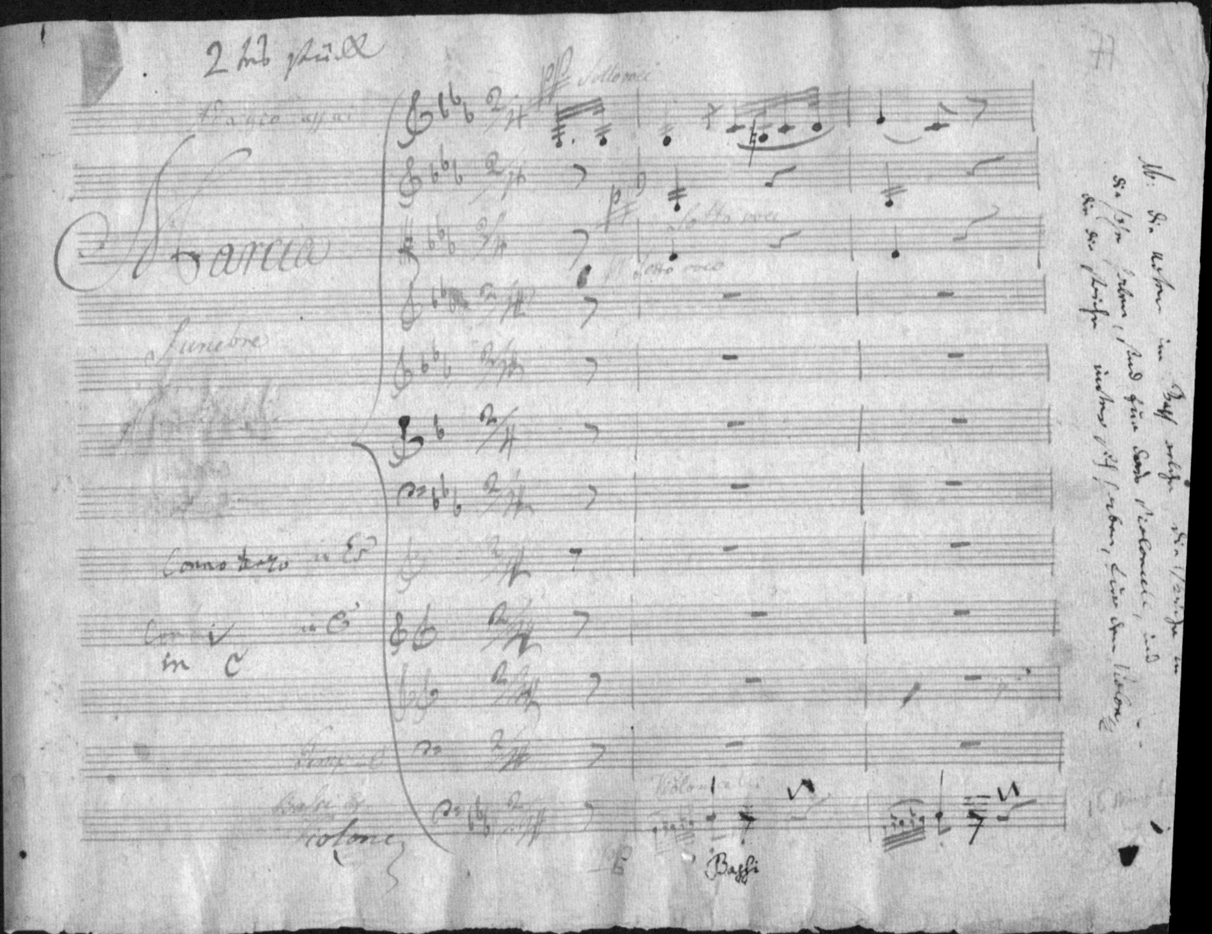
Marcia
funebre
Corno terzo in Es
in C
sotto voce
Bassi

[Here] Beethoven has a wicked trick for the horn. A few bars before the complete theme is restated Beethoven has the horn play it while the violins are still playing the chord of the second. For someone who is unfamiliar with the score this always gives the impression that the horn player has miscounted and come in too early. However, during the first rehearsal of this symphony, which went appallingly, the horn player came in correctly. I was standing next to Beethoven and, thinking it was wrong, I said, 'That damned horn player! Can't he count properly? It sounds horrible!' I think I nearly got my ears boxed. Beethoven did not forgive me for a long time.[3]

The annotated first page of Beethoven's manuscript fair copy of the *Eroica*'s second movement, the Funeral March. It is curious that he should have written the word 'Marcia' in large and florid penmanship with the much smaller 'funebre' tacked on below – it almost as an afterthought.

Ries was scarcely to be blamed, for Beethoven was throwing away the rule book of harmony and creating his own. It might be hard to believe today, but in the nineteenth century editors and conductors often took it upon themselves to 'correct' this passage in both print and performance.

The coda at the end of this monumental first movement also breaks both usage and rules. Audiences were used to the Classical composers' little codettas at the end of a movement (such as the four bars that end the slow movement of Haydn's B flat major String Quartet, Op. 55 No. 3, or the ten bars that round off the last movement of Mozart's B flat major Piano Sonata, K. 333/315c). They would also have adapted to the more recent and imposing endings of certain symphonies. The 83 bars that end Haydn's 'London' Symphony in D major (No. 104) of 1795 contain 8 extraordinary bars (293–300) whose widening leaps for the strings vividly show how very indebted Beethoven was to his old teacher. Not only does he write some almost identical string passages in this first movement of the 'Eroica', but he has learned the possibilities

The manuscript of Beethoven's
earlier Funeral March On the
Death of a Hero: the slow
movement of the Piano Sonata
in A flat Op. 26 of 1800–1. This
was one of the pieces played by
the band that accompanied his
coffin to Währing cemetery in
1827.

a coda could be made to offer. Listeners would have been stunned by Beethoven's 140 bars of magnificent originality that end this first movement. Far from acting as a decorous and allusive full stop, his coda is practically a movement on its own, beginning with another of his coups that were to be notorious before they became famous. This was to restate the main theme in three abrupt downward steps in the successive keys of E flat, D flat and C without any modulations in between to soften the harshness. And once again, heard against the background of what has gone before and heretical as it is in terms of contemporary musical orthodoxy, the device simply *sounds* right.

II *MARCIA FUNEBRE – ADAGIO ASSAI*

Any work of art, no matter how novel, has both a historical context and antecedents. As already noted, in Vienna in the 1790s Beethoven would have been familiar with the occasional music written for French revolutionary festivals, much of it marches in 4/4 time. It was self-consciously 'new' music to suit the new society the Revolution had supposedly declared, and it had travelled all over Europe. It would be surprising had Beethoven not picked up some musical tricks from it, whether unconsciously or deliberately, even if the overwhelming originality of the 'Eroica' now seems to eclipse everything that went before it, extinguishing rather than embodying whatever immediate models it might have had.

Marcia funebre sulla morte d'un Eroe.

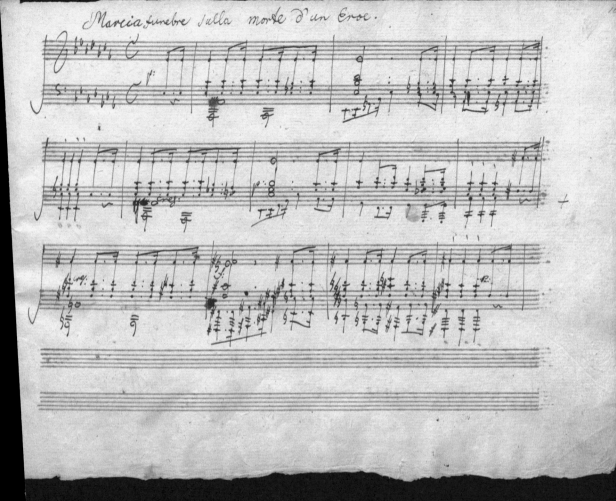

Academics have certainly not been slow to look for traces of the music associated with the French Revolution in the 'Eroica', and anyone with a determined thesis of musical influence will always manage to find parallels. In receptive minds melodies recur and leave behind their echoes. There might simply be a chance similarity between two tunes, or a scholar might conduct a laborious analysis to reveal a 'hidden text' of the same notes that purportedly lies behind both. As a teenage viola player in the Bonn theatre orchestra at the time of the Revolution Beethoven would have played the popular operatic repertoire, which at the time included works by contemporary French composers such as Grétry, Monsigny, Dalayrac (he had the scores of two of Dalayrac's operas in his library), Le Sueur, Méhul and above all Gossec.

François-Joseph Gossec (1734–1829) was perhaps the Revolution's foremost composer. Among his many 'political' works were the *Symphonie militaire* and the widely known *Marche lugubre* (1790). This slow march was played on solemn occasions such as the funeral of a national figure. It accompanied the grand public ceremony when the remains of Voltaire and Rousseau were moved to the Panthéon. It is practically certain that Beethoven knew the piece, if not from Bonn then early on in Vienna. It was chromatic, made use of dramatic effects such as long pauses, and was scored for unusual instruments including tam-tam, serpent, muted drum and a special tuba. The late American musicologist Claude V. Palisca singled out a passage in the second movement of the 'Eroica', the *Marcia* *funebre*, where Beethoven appears almost to parody a passage in Gossec's *Marche lugubre.*[*]

Without consulting the composer it is impossible to say whether or not this was sheer coincidence. The one certain thing is that it was not plagiarism. Beethoven was far too original and jealous of his own musical fecundity to need to crib other composers' music. Similarly, the slow march at the beginning of Cherubini's *Hymne funèbre sur la mort du Général Hoche* (1797) has been proposed as another influence.

In any case it was a great time for grand orchestral funeral marches. Yet another was the slow movement of Paul Wranitzky's C minor Symphony, Op. 31, written in 1797 with the subtitle *Grande sinfonie caractéristique pour la paix avec la République françoise*. Wranitzky, who shared Mozart's birth year of 1756, was a major figure in the musical life of Vienna as a composer, conductor and violinist. As a measure of the respect in which Wranitzky was held, Haydn insisted that he direct Viennese performances of *The Creation* in 1799 and 1800, while Beethoven himself chose him to conduct the premiere of the First Symphony in April 1800. However, the first performance in Vienna of Wranitzky's own C minor Symphony had been quickly banned by imperial decree, because its French subtitle was considered inflammatory. The work was full of musical allusions to the French Revolution, including in its first movement various quotations from Cherubini's opera *Médée*: an opera with a reputedly subversive

---

*   See Appendix, p. 185.

message. The quotations from Haydn in Wranitzky's symphony were also taken to represent the Austro-Hungarian Empire's fuddy-duddy old regime confronted by the triumphant new republicanism sweeping Europe. Significantly, the symphony's slow movement was a funeral march in C minor, exactly prefiguring the one in the 'Eroica', although Wranitzky's is a lament for 'the Fate and Death of Louis XVI' rather than for Napoleon.

Beethoven, too, had provided his own precedent for this most solemn of slow movements: that of his A flat major Piano Sonata, Op. 26, written some two years before the 'Eroica'. This was titled *Marcia funebre sulla morte d'un eroe* and marked *Maestoso andante*. Set in the uncommon key of A flat minor (rather than in the relative minor, F minor) it is indebted to French antecedents in that it is a proper slow march with dotted rhythms that keep the pulse going. It has a brief central section that mimics orchestral effects, including the dramatic pauses that also characterized the French genre. In the wrong hands it can risk sounding throwaway and even faintly ludicrous. It is impossible to say how consciously Beethoven had had Bonaparte in mind as the 'hero' in question when writing it. However, it is probably safe to say that at that time, shortly after the Battle of Marengo when the Austrians had been so decisively driven out of Italy, any generic hero would be bound to have cast a Napoleonic shadow.

In the context of this symphony we can assume the hero so imposingly called forth in the first movement is now dead, even if at the start the music is perhaps too stately and 'public' to induce personal grief. The key is C minor, which Beethoven has already established in works such as the *Pathétique* Sonata as having private associations of somewhat histrionic passion, if not always of actual lament. As the movement proceeds, however, there are moments that go straight to the heart, above all the episode in C major that comforts, as the music-ologist George Grove wrote, like a sudden ray of sunlight in a dark sky. All too short, it gives way to the original march, which then turns into a solemn fugue for full orchestra, the stately progress of which becomes briefly impassioned before the music resumes its deep-purple march and shuffles to a close.

If there is anything in this movement that betrays French influence it is its aura of having been conceived for a great public ceremony. It is not by accident that it has so frequently been trotted out for moments of national mourning (for John F. Kennedy, for example). Indeed, it is quite hard for us to hear it any longer as just the slow movement of a symphony. It would doubtless have delighted Beethoven that it so readily conjures images of cenotaphs, black crape, slow-marching soldiers, gun carriages, riderless horses with reversed boots in the stirrups (a particularly vulgar and sentimental piece of theatre), and all the rest of the panoply of militarized national mourning for a civilian. He was plainly aiming for a grand epitome of public grief, and an epitome is exactly what he triumphantly achieved.

III SCHERZO: ALLEGRO VIVACE

What are we to make of Beethoven's following a funeral dead march with a 'joke' (a scherzo)? In the early Viennese Classical period this movement of a symphony was a simple and stately three-beats-to-the-bar minuet. Thereafter, Haydn and Mozart made it bear more weight, and it had tended to become quicker and more complex until most symphonic 'minuet' movements had long since abandoned any connection with dancing. Haydn had increasingly used 'scherzo' when indicating a particularly light-hearted version of this movement, especially in a string quartet.

Beethoven had long adopted this marking with enthusiasm, as in the rollicking third movement of his First Symphony although, unlike Haydn's, his scherzos were often less urbanely witty than downright knockabout. After the monumental first two movements of the 'Eroica', though, his problem was how to effect a change of mood without destroying the overall tone of seriousness. The shift in rhythm from the slow movement's four-beats-in-a-bar march to a more lilting three undoubtedly brings relief, but Beethoven then needed to write a movement that was reinvigorating and, above all, without the least hint of anything frivolous.

One dawn in a far-off land many years ago I was woken by a cock crow that instantly put the *Scherzo* of the 'Eroica' into my head for the rest of the day. The bird's high, almost trilling clarion note followed by a downward glissando was so distinctive I have wondered ever since if Beethoven had once heard just such a cockerel (in the days when he still could), and the heraldic cry had lingered in his unconscious as an aural metaphor for the awakening and regeneration of a new day. Such speculation can be pushed too far, but it does seem appropriate that after the first seven bars in which the strings (marked *sempre pianissimo e staccato*) softly climb an octave like a sun rising in obvious expectation, Beethoven gives the 'cock crow' to the oboes – his orchestra's most gallinaceous sound.

Once this day has dawned, though, and the implications dissected (still *pianissimo*) among different instruments, the full orchestra gathers itself and explodes with the call, *fortissimo*. After the hero's solemn obsequies it is impossible not to see this as signalling a triumphant rebirth. Proof of what Beethoven could do with the notes of the common chord of E flat major is once more shown when the orchestra twice plays in unison a passage in which the stress falls onto the weak beat:

This sort of syncopation was already a favourite device of Beethoven's. It might indeed pass as jocular, except that the lightness of the remainder of this first half of the movement, with strings and wind alternating, makes it more playful than humorous. There follows the trio section with the famous three horns mellifluously giving their private version of the common chord of E flat major. In those pre-valve days of the hand-stopped 'natural' horn such a flourish would almost inevitably have been associated with a hunting motif: the stock trope of so many works of the Classical period. Beethoven manages to sidestep this by writing reflective rather than rousing music, and when the passage recurs in the trio's second half the unaccompanied three horns die away with long-held chords that are deeply affecting. When writing about this in 1896, George Grove wondered what it was that made these last few notes so touching. 'There is in them a feeling of infinitude or eternity such as is conveyed by no other passage, even in Beethoven's music', he said and went on to quote Wordsworth:

Our destiny, our being's heart and home
Is with infinitude, and only there;
With hope it is, hope that can never die,
Effort, and expectation, and desire,
And something evermore about to be.[4]

Such mystical overtones were undoubtedly Beethoven's answer to anyone who might have assumed a scherzo automatically meant a jest. When the syncopated unison passage of the trio's first half recurs in the second, he changes not the notes but the rhythm in a masterstroke of inventiveness. Both syncopation and 3/4 time are abandoned, and in their place the full orchestra suddenly has an electrifying 4 fortissimo bars in duple time:

The movement ends with equally loud emphatic chords. Yet an impression of infinitude still lingers, or at any rate of an inward horizon expansive enough still to justify the massive portal that opened the symphony. In its way, even the *Scherzo* is as monumental as the rest.

IV FINALE: ALLEGRO MOLTO

How to end a serious composition was always a problem for composers of the Viennese Classical period. It was somehow implicit in the age of sonata form that no matter how earnest a work's mood, it ought to have the musical equivalent of a happy ending. Obviously Church works such as Bach's Passions could leave their hearers if not actually depressed then at least suitably meditative. But in secular instrumental music there was a widespread feeling that the ending should be distinctly lighter, and it often took the form of a rondo with a catchy recurring tune. It was not really until the Romantics that composers felt free leave their listeners luxuriating in gloom.

This was obviously unsatisfactory at times, the contrast with what had gone before sounding merely flippant. A classic case is Mozart's String Quintet in G minor, K. 516, a work redolent of private sorrow all the way through to the last movement, whose short *Adagio* introduction in G minor is probably the most depressed passage Mozart ever wrote. Yet this breaks off into a jaunty tune in the major key in 6/8 time. According to taste, the sudden contrast is either ill judged or utterly heartbreaking.

Probably the first great composer of the Viennese Classical period to make a serious intellectual attempt to solve the dilemma was Haydn in his set of six string quartets, Op. 20, the so-called 'Sun' quartets, which constitute a landmark in a genre that he himself had invented. Written in 1772, they were plainly designed to be a great advance on his previous set, Op. 17, and serious enough in tone to stand on an equal footing with any other instrumental genre. In order that their last movements could maintain this tone, Haydn chose to end three of them with fugues: a forcible injection of the old-fashioned 'learned' mode into the sonata form style. The irony was that sonata form had originally evolved expressly to free music from all that Bachian counterpoint. Haydn's novel solution was reasonably successful, certainly enough for Mozart to copy the idea in the finale of his own D minor String Quartet, K. 173, of 1773. Eventually this pattern was modified by both composers, as well as by many others, into a fusion that blended fugal passages into the more 'normal' Viennese Classical finale. The result was something that could be both lyrical and thoughtful: a solution later to be exploited by Beethoven and Mendelssohn.

As we already know, when Beethoven came to tackle the problem in the 'Eroica' of how to follow three epic movements with something that would not be an anti-climax he resorted to his 'Prometheus' theme for a set of variations with a fugal section. Because the movement is now imprinted at near-genetic level in generations of audiences, it is impossible to imagine it any differently. The 'Prometheus' theme has virtually become the symphony's signature tune. Yet from the earliest performances there were always those who felt this last movement was by a hair's breadth not quite up to the impact of the other three. Possibly it was because the idea of having a theme and variations as its last movement was the one thing in this symphony that struck listeners as less original than the rest. By the time Beethoven came to write the 'Eroica' there were some brilliant examples of variations being put to use for both light-hearted and serious finales, especially by Mozart in such examples as his C minor Wind Serenade, K. 388, of 1782 and several of his piano concertos, including the G major, K. 453, and Beethoven's own favourite, the C minor, K. 491 of 1786.

Like the Op. 35 piano variations, the last movement of the 'Eroica' begins with the identical naked bass line being gradually fleshed out until the 'Prometheus' theme stands proud. Thereafter the theme is varied in different ways but seamlessly and with a good deal of effortless-sounding fugato and counterpoint. It is impressive that this is not merely an orchestration of the piano work. The treatment is fresh and different, a tribute to the possibilities for a composer of Beethoven's resourcefulness of what had once been a little dance tune. At one point the music slows for a section marked *Poco andante* where an oboe tune of great expressiveness is introduced:

This gradually suffuses the whole orchestra and clearly harks back to the funeral music of the slow movement, thereby invoking a unity between the dead and the resurgent hero. Then the music regains its former pace before breaking into a hectic fast tempo that ends the symphony in triumph. The trinity of Prometheus, Bonaparte and Beethoven reigns supreme: all achieved in a few weeks by a deaf musician scratching away in 1803 with ink and quills in an upstairs room whose casements were thrown open on an Austrian landscape in high summer. The crisis of Heiligenstadt has been vanquished. The promises of Bonn have been heapingly fulfilled. A stake has finally been driven through the heart of 'Papa' Haydn, even though he has another six years to live. A symphony that will ring down the centuries has been written.

6

WHO WAS THE REAL HERO OF THE 'EROICA'?

In the first three decades of the nineteenth century there were three men who fitted the near-mythological status of Romantic hero. They were Napoleon, Beethoven and Byron: flawed and lonely geniuses who were seen as having lived heroic lives and made heroic deaths still with their ideals intact. The little Corsican's myth continued to dominate Europe even after he was exiled to St Helena following Waterloo in 1815. The 'Napoleonic' character clearly transcended the man and his career. Similarly, the 'Byronic' myth transcended Byron, his brilliant and prodigious output as a writer, his scandalous love affairs, and the political adventuring that in 1824 led to his death at the age of thirty-six while fighting for Greece against the Ottoman Empire.

As for Beethoven, the academic John Clubbe notes, 'At first glance it might appear that [he] admired the republican Napoleon, inheritor of the French Revolution, and despised the royal Napoleon, emperor and despot. But in fact B's feelings, like Byron's, were ambivalent and fluctuated wildly over the years.'[1] Even back in Bonn it is likely that Beethoven was planning a piece of music inspired by the idea of Napoleon, although not necessarily in any obvious programmatic sense. As we know, it was Bonaparte's embodiment as the agent of liberating change that attracted him as it attracted thousands of others: the idea of Europe's peoples at last being freed of servitude to kings and princes, bishops and priests. This, to Beethoven, would have been the true spirit of the times, and Napoleon happened to be its incarnation. It is easy today to underestimate the effect on some of Europe's greatest minds of what swiftly became thought of as *Bonapartism*: an idea that had grown out of the Enlightenment to occupy an imaginative space somewhere between ideology and hero worship. In a modern sense Napoleon had gone beyond mere celebrity to achieve stardom, and intellectuals and writers including Kant, Hegel, Schiller and Goethe were ardent fans.

All the same, it is too simple to take at face value Beethoven's intention to dedicate his Third Symphony to Bonaparte, as it overlooks the muddle of complex and even conflicting motives that lay behind it. A century and a half of programme notes has led audiences to search the music for expressions of various portentous abstract nouns such as Triumph, Will, Humanity, Freedom and even Revolutionary Fervour, dating back to the fateful events in Paris of 1789. *Humanity* in particular was a quality many intellectual children of the Enlightenment loosely associated with Bonapartism, in ironic disregard of the Terror and the subsequent battlefield slaughters that actually made Napoleon's name. It supposedly betokened sacrifice, service and social loyalty towards a mankind whose most abject guttersnipe was theoretically of equal value to a prince. Wordsworth, who as a young man initially fell beneath the Bonapartist spell, famously wrote of the 'still, sad music of humanity' in his 1798 poem on Tintern Abbey. (Cynics will note how very much easier it is to shed a tear over Humanity in the abstract than it can be to sustain devotion to an individual through thick and thin.) Yet such grand nouns are often hard for a modern audience to associate with a particular work of art, whether a poem such as *The Prelude* or a symphony such as the 'Eroica', even though Beethoven himself frequently thought in such terms. It is perfectly reasonable to hear the 'Eroica' simply as an extraordinary aesthetic achievement whose true revolutionary nature was entirely musical. Yet understanding some of its Bonapartist antecedents adds much interest.

None knew better than the composer himself just how ground-breaking his new symphony was, and he realized it ought to be performed in Vienna before he took it with him to France as he was still planning. Given the length of its first movement, in particular, he needed to reassure himself that his intuition about matters of timing and balance was correct. A trial run was essential, and Prince Lobkowitz's excellent private orchestra would be ideal for the purpose. On 22 October 1803 Beethoven's pupil Ferdinand Ries wrote once more to the publisher Nikolaus Simrock saying that Beethoven very much wanted to dedicate the symphony to Bonaparte. However, Lobkowitz had already offered the composer 400 ducats for the symphony's rights for half a year: a munificent offer that Beethoven could not afford to turn down. The snag was that the prince was a deeply patriotic Austrian and in the circumstances it would have been fatal for Beethoven to stick to his original plan of making Napoleon its dedicatee with the Corsican's name prominent on the title page.

Born in Bonn fourteen years after Beethoven, Ferdinand Ries went to Vienna in October 1801 where he was welcomed by Beethoven as his pupil and sometime secretary. He was a talented musician. As a native of Bonn he became liable to French conscription and was summoned back in 1805 even though he had lost an eye to smallpox in childhood which disbarred him from military service. The anonymous portraitist presumably restored his eye for aesthetic reasons.

Beethoven was quite capable of making pragmatic business decisions, which is why he judiciously dedicated the 'Eroica' to Prince Lobkowitz while retaining its general title of *'Bonaparte'*. Between the work's completion in the late summer of 1803 and the score's publication in October 1806 Austria's Francophobia was further intensified by external political events such as the series of crushing defeats the Austrian army suffered in 1806 that led to Napoleon himself taking up residence in Vienna's Schönbrunn Palace in November that year after Francis II and his court had fled. By then, too, Beethoven's original Bonapartist leanings had evaporated, particularly after the news reached Vienna in May 1804 that France's self-appointed first consul had now declared himself emperor. Ferdinand Ries recorded this celebrated incident:

In this symphony Beethoven had Bonaparte in mind, but as he was when he was First Consul. Beethoven esteemed him greatly at the time and likened him to the greatest Roman consuls. I as well as several of his more intimate friends saw a copy of the score lying upon his table with the word 'Buonaparte' at the extreme top of the title page, and at the extreme bottom 'Luigi van Beethoven', but not another word. Whether and with what the space between was to be filled out, I do not know. I was the first to bring him the intelligence that Buonaparte had proclaimed himself emperor, whereupon he flew into a rage and cried out: 'Is he then, too, nothing more than an ordinary human being? Now he, too, will trample on all the rights of man and indulge only his ambition. He will exalt himself above all others, become a tyrant!' Beethoven went to the table, took hold of the title page by the top, tore it in two, and threw it on the floor. The page was rewritten and only then did the symphony receive the title Sinfonia eroica.[2]

No doubt at this moment the disillusioned Beethoven would have agreed with his contemporary, William Blake, that

The strongest poison ever known
Came from Caesar's laurel crown

as he would with Blake's 'I will not Reason & Compare; my business is to Create.'

Barely a month after this outburst the first, semi-public trial run of the symphony by Lobkowitz's palace orchestra took place at an overlong 'Academy' with a programme of other challenging Beethoven works and after gruelling all-day rehearsals. Opinions were mixed, but on balance they were favourable even if, as the audience staggered out punch drunk into the warm Viennese night, a good many probably felt they would rather like not to hear another note of new music for quite some time. Two months later, in August, Beethoven told the publisher Härtel that the symphony's actual title was 'Bonaparte'. Did this mean his fit of rage in May over the self-proclaimed new emperor had been no more than a typically Beethovenish fury of the moment, or was it part of an increasingly ambivalent attitude towards Napoleon that was shared by many others?

We know that by the time Beethoven was at work on the symphony in Oberdöbling in the early summer of 1803, his adolescent enthusiasm for the French Revolution had considerably ebbed.* Nor was he alone in his pessimism. Those early years of the nineteenth century witnessed a painful reassessment of Napoleon and post-revolutionary France by many in Europe and particularly by German-speaking intellectuals. The Enlightenment had been enormously influential, and in terms of its complex interleaving of meaning and ideas, Beethoven's 'Eroica' can be viewed as having something in common with certain German non-musical works of the time, such as Goethe's *Faust*, Jean Paul's proto-Romantic novels (that were to so entrance Schumann as a youth), Hegel's philosophy (the section entitled 'Absolute Freedom and Terror' in *The Phenomenology of Mind*) and even Caspar David Friedrich's paintings. But in the face of Bonaparte's military conquests, pragmatic deals and his army's increasing threat to German-speaking territory, much of the Germans' former idealism had vanished to be replaced by an upsurge in nationalism. By 1805 Beethoven, in common with many intellectuals (including Jean Paul, Hegel and Caspar David Friedrich), had become more of a German patriot and

Prince Louis Ferdinand of Prussia, a nephew of Frederick the Great, was two years younger than Beethoven, a piano virtuoso and a composer of considerable originality. He greatly admired Beethoven, whom he befriended on terms of complete social equality. His death in 1806 at the Battle of Saalfeld when he was only thirty-four made him a hero in Austria and further boosted the growing Francophobia of the Germanic world.

---

*   See Chapter 3, p. 67.

Johann Nepomuk Hummel (1778–1837) as painted by an unknown artist around 1814. He was a composer and virtuoso pianist who had been a pupil of Mozart's. In Vienna he was considered Beethoven's only real rival as an improviser until Beethoven's deafness overtook him. In 1810 Hummel fell out with Beethoven over a disparaging remark about that composer's Mass in C but paid a visit to the great man's sickbed in 1827.

even somewhat Francophobic. By March 1806 when a revised version of *Fidelio* was successfully launched in Vienna, the opera was widely understood by audiences as having an anti-French message, with Florestan in his lowest dungeon representing a Germanic world in dire need of rescue by a faithful Leonora, whether or not cross-dressed as 'Fidelio'.

With all this in mind, how are we to construe the wording of the 'Eroica' Symphony's title page when it was finally published in October 1806? The Italian inscription ran *Sinfonia eroica / composta per festiggiare il souvenir di un grand Uomo*, and it is nearly always taken for granted that the '*grand Uomo*' is Napoleon. Certainly the surviving and much amended title page of the original manuscript bears Beethoven's own inscription in pencil: '*geschrieben auf Bonaparte*', although this has its own ambiguity. The '*auf*' could imply something done in someone's name or in their honour, or it could just mean 'on' as in the title of an essay or a poem (Montaigne's 'On Solitude' or Auden's 'On Sunday Walks'). Beethoven's 'On Napoleon', then?

A fresh theory has emerged that proposes a quite different and plausible identity for the *grand Uomo*.[3] After Napoleon's resounding defeat of the Austrians and Russians at Austerlitz in December 1805 the Prussian army came in for heavy criticism for having abandoned its allies to their fate. Those closest to the Prussian king, Frederick William III, pleaded with him to avenge Austerlitz. They argued that the Prussian army should confront the upstart Napoleon anywhere on

German territory. Foremost among those putting this case was the young Prince Louis Ferdinand.

Louis Ferdinand was a quite exceptional character. A nephew of Frederick the Great, he was a hopeless spendthrift and an authentic military hero in his own right, having already fought the French in several engagements and won widespread acclaim for his fearless leadership on the battlefield. At the same time he was also a first-rate musician and virtuoso pianist who had studied under Jan Ladislav Dussek. Beethoven had first met him on a visit to Berlin in 1796. The two had become friends, and Beethoven, the prince's elder by two years and probably at the peak of his own brilliance as a pianist, reckoned Louis Ferdinand a better pianist even than Hummel: by implication second only to himself. The prince was also a composer of considerable originality and Beethoven evidently felt he had found a kindred spirit.

Quite how original a musician Louis Ferdinand was can best be gauged by the way his music would be championed by a later generation. Perhaps the composition that made the biggest impact was his Piano Quartet in F minor, Op. 6 (1806), his last work. Schumann's diaries reveal an abiding interest in both the prince, whose music he studied in depth, and this piece. He wrote a set of piano variations for four hands on a theme from the quartet, now unfortunately lost. Schumann was also inspired by Louis Ferdinand's exploration of unusual combinations of instruments such as in his *Notturno*, Op. 8, for piano, flute, violin, cello and two French horns. Clara

Wieck, Schumann's pianist wife, took part in a performance of the F minor Piano Quartet at which Mendelssohn was present and all agreed that Louis Ferdinand had been a composer before his time, a true proto-Romantic. The markings on the score of this piece were far more numerous and expressive than was customary at the turn of the nineteenth century: *con anima, dolcissimo, smorzando, con passione, con molta forca* [*sic*], *con duolo*: very much the sort of indications that were to become fashionable only later. Nor was it until the Romantic era that composers felt free to end their pieces on a hushed note. The prince had no qualms about letting the music of his piano quartet, already very dark and turbulent, die away (*morendo*) in shadows, ending with two soft *pizzicato* chords for strings alone. Not for him an upbeat Classical ending. Like Schumann, the arch-Romantic Franz Liszt was also deeply impressed by this piano quartet and in 1847 wrote an *Elégie sur des motifs du Prince Ferdinand de Prusse*.

But such accolades and homage lay far in the future. In 1804, while en route to Italy, Prince Louis Ferdinand stayed with Beethoven's patron Prince Lobkowitz at his castle in Raudnitz (today's Roudnice) north of Prague. Louis Ferdinand must have asked what Beethoven had been writing lately, and as the proud dedicatee of the 'Eroica' Lobkowitz had his orchestra play the new symphony. By now the players knew the music well, having already given its first performances. At the end Louis Ferdinand excitedly asked to hear the 'Eroica' a second time, and Lobkowitz happily obliged. When that was

The Lichnowsky Palace, known locally as the White Castle of Grätz in Hradec, today's Czech Republic. It was here in 1806 that Beethoven came with his patron Prince Karl Lichnowsky, a visit (and a friendship) brought to a premature end by Beethoven's storming out over some perceived slight and making his own way back to Vienna.

over the young prince wanted to hear it yet again. Lobkowitz insisted his orchestra should be given a rest and dinner before the tired players embarked on a third consecutive performance of the entire symphony, which they duly gave. It is unclear whether Beethoven was also present on this occasion but it seems likely that he was. Whatever else, the episode was eloquent testimony to Louis Ferdinand's seriousness both as a musician and an admirer of Beethoven. What is certain is that both men renewed their friendship at this time and at least on one occasion the prince wined and dined Beethoven on terms of absolute equality, seated next to him at table (in those days an unthinkable solecism for a scruffy commoner like Beethoven). That his Third Piano Concerto had been dedicated to Louis Ferdinand is surely a mark of Beethoven's esteem for this sensitive and accomplished prince.

Meanwhile, Napoleon Bonaparte was once again making himself impossible to ignore in Austria, and on 19 October 1805 the Austrian general Karl Mack lost his entire army to Napoleon at Ulm, after which nothing stood in the way of the French advance into central Europe. French troops captured Vienna in November 1805 and a month later achieved a crushing defeat of the forces of the Holy Roman Empire at the Battle of Austerlitz. Under acute pressure the following August Francis II dissolved the Holy Roman Empire and abdicated. That same month in 1806 Beethoven was staying with his friend and patron Prince Lichnowsky at his family's castle at Grätz, 150 miles from Vienna in today's Czech

Republic.. One night the Prince asked him to play the piano for some visiting French officers and Beethoven truculently refused, saying that he wasn't a servant to obey orders. Whether this was because the officers were French or it was just another flare-up in his often stormy relationship with Lichnowsky is not clear, but it escalated into a shouting match and allegedly a Count Oppersdorff only just managed to prevent Beethoven breaking a chair over his princely patron's head. Beethoven left the castle in a fury there and then, arriving back ill in Vienna after a miserable three-day journey in carts and coaches, during which he and his trunk were soaked in a rainstorm, the water damage still clearly visible on the manuscript of the 'Appassionata' Sonata he was carrying with him.

The significance of this episode in the autumn of 1806 is that it was most likely at Grätz that Beethoven learned that his friend and fellow musician Prince Louis Ferdinand had been killed a few days earlier on 10 October at the Battle of Saalfeld, a preliminary skirmish before yet another crushing French victory at nearby Jena. On the last evening of his life the prince had performed his friend Dussek's Double Piano Concerto, Op. 63. On the battlefield next day he spurned a French soldier's offer of surrender and was duly run through. He was thirty-four. On 29 October in an article of deep mourning the *Wiener Zeitung* announced a forthcoming tribute edition of practically all the prince's music. In the same issue the newspaper also gave notice of the first publication of the 'Eroica' Symphony and included the wording of Beethoven's

A characteristic Beethoven manuscript: a page of the Appassionata Sonata showing the ravages of his wet journey back from Hradec. The passage shown is of bars 134-157 of the last movement. If he had brought this manuscript with him in 1806 it seems likely he was still working on it. The sonata was finally published the following year.

final Italian inscription on the title page. By then Beethoven was back in Vienna, no doubt still furious with Lichnowsky and the French and grieving for his heroic and talented friend. He could judge better than anyone the loss to music. The theory advanced by the German musicologist Peter Schleuning is that the '*grand Uomo*' of his symphony's new inscription is not Bonaparte at all but the gifted musician and dashing warrior slain by Napoleon's troops, thus turning the 'Eroica' into a musical expression of German patriotism.[4] If so, Beethoven could never have made this public. It would have compromised the symphony's existing dedication to Prince Lobkowitz by implying that it honoured a greater man than the patron who had loyally stood by Beethoven with financial support. And revealing the great man to have been a Prussian prince rather than Napoleon could ruin the chances of the symphony ever selling in French-dominated Europe.

Whatever the truth, it is clear that Beethoven's feelings about Napoleon were as mixed as everybody else's and, like theirs, could border on the obsessive. However, when it comes to appreciating the 'Eroica', it is probably best not to attach too much importance to the connection with Bonaparte and certainly not to imagine the French emperor's shadowy figure looming behind the score in his white waistcoat and braided coat and bicorne hat. It was still unclear what Beethoven really felt when he learned of his erstwhile hero's death on St Helena in May 1821. Asked whether he might perhaps write some sort of requiem for him, Beethoven merely replied, 'I have already composed the proper music for that catastrophe.'[5] Presumably this referred to the *Funeral March* of the 'Eroica', but it might equally well have meant the entire symphony or, indeed, his own life's work. In 1824 he remarked to his ex-pupil and friend Carl Czerny, 'Once upon a time I couldn't bear Napoleon. Now I think quite differently.'

7

THE RECEPTION OF THE 'EROICA'

As we have seen, Beethoven's new symphony was launched with a handful of semi-public performances by the private orchestra of its dedicatee, Prince Lobkowitz. It is certain that by today's standards these would have been fairly painful affairs for the hearers. Neither of Beethoven's previous two symphonies had proved easy to play, but the challenges of the 'Eroica' were in a league of their own. This was no average eighteenth-century chamber work, which would have been well within the players' scope by being shorter, with fewer excursions into unfamiliar keys, with more musical clichés giving opportunities for playing on autopilot, and generally more predictable in every sense. That being said, the number of instruments needed for the 'Eroica' was not much greater than was required for Mozart's late G minor Symphony, a performance of which in Baron van Swieten's house with the composer present was so distressingly bad that Mozart reportedly had to leave the room. The raggedness of an orchestra naturally tended to increase with the number of instruments and the difficulty of the music, and it was really only in the second decade of the nineteenth century, when symphonists such as Beethoven had nourished a fashion for ever-larger ensembles, that the role of a separate conductor for an orchestra became established as a matter of course and out of real necessity. With few exceptions the tradition of a continuo player leading from a keyboard had barely outlived the eighteenth century, and a member of the orchestra – usually the Konzertmeister (the leader of the first violins) –

would indicate the time in the trickier places by waving his bow. Beethoven's own interventions as a conductor in the rehearsals for the 'Eroica' were disastrous and muddled still further players already at sea in his difficult work. Complete breakdowns and restarts were frequent.

A related problem was the sheer size of the programmes that were undertaken in Beethoven's day, some of which seem almost to have been calculated to guarantee indifferent performances. One such was the concert of his own works that Beethoven himself had organized at the Theater an der Wien on 5 April 1803, a mere two months before he took up residence in Oberdöbling and began serious work on the 'Eroica':

The programme contained the First and Second Symphonies, the Piano Concerto in C minor (soloist Beethoven) and the first performance of the oratorio Christus am Oelberge. It began at 8 a.m.; by 2.30 everyone was exhausted and angry. But for dear, kind Prince Lichnowsky. . . the day would have been a fiasco. He it was who thoughtfully provided baskets of bread and butter, meat and wine, fed the hungry men and persuaded them to try again. Even then the oratorio was not a great success. For once the crowd instinct was right: Beethoven had misjudged his style, as he himself admitted later.[1]

Only the previous year Beethoven had confided in a friend, the violinist Wenzel Krumpholz, that he was dissatisfied with his works so far. 'From today', he said, 'I intend to take a new road.' The 'Eroica' was therefore Beethoven's first symphony in what he thought of as his new style.

The first proper review was of a performance in January 1805 and appeared in the *Allgemeine musikalische Zeitung* on 13 February. The reviewer began ominously with a gushing eulogy of Beethoven's First Symphony as 'a glorious work of art' with 'an extraordinary wealth of lovely ideas treated in the most splendid and graceful style, with coherence, order and clarity reigning throughout'. Having established this point of comparison he put the boot in. In essence, he said, this new Third Symphony was

a daring, wild fantasy of inordinate length and extremely difficult to play. There is no lack of striking and beautiful passages in which the composer's power and talent are obvious; but often the work seems to lose itself in utter confusion. It begins with a powerfully scored Allegro in E flat, followed by a Funeral March in C minor, treated fugally towards the end. … This writer belongs to Beethoven's warmest admirers, but in the present work he finds very much that is odd and harsh that enormously increases the difficulty of understanding the music and almost completely obscuring its unity.[2]

The same critic was still more dismissive of another performance in April, this time criticizing the symphony's inordinate length, recommending that Beethoven shorten it and saying it had lasted 'a full hour', which does suggest much slower tempi than would be usual today. The performance he was referring to took place in the Theater an der Wien and was the work's true public premiere, which the composer himself, now very deaf, conducted with a flurry of distracting gestures and ferocious glares. It was scarcely a triumph. The orchestra

The title page of the autograph full score of the 'Eroica' with Beethoven's emendations and remarks. It is clearly dated 'In August 1804'. Under 'Sinfonia Grande' scholarship has revealed the scratched-out words 'Intitulata Bonaparte'. Beethoven's faint pencil scrawls beneath his own name read 'Geschrieben auf Bonaparte' and were never erased.

was as much at sea as the audience, and at one point the pianist–composer Carl Czerny heard the heartfelt cry from the gallery of a man who, no doubt bitterly thinking of his entrance fee, shouted in exasperation, 'I'd give another Kreutzer if only it would *stop!*' Baffled as many of Beethoven's listeners might have been, they probably would not have gone as far as the wise men of Prague Conservatory a little later who, when the 'Eroica' was performed there, declared it 'morally depraved' (*ein sittenverderbendes Werk*). Nor did it help the symphony's immediate reception that it was not finally published until 1806, which made the parts more accessible and reliable than those transcribed by copyists. After that, with one or two notable exceptions, its fame and acceptance grew rapidly the more it was heard.

All the same, there was at the time no lack of dissenting voices of those who thought the 'Eroica' was an incoherent din, and some people just never did acquire a taste for Beethoven, who seemed to them to grow ever more outlandish, his late works being quite impenetrable. George Onslow (1784–1853), a French composer with an English father, said in an interview with Joseph d'Ortigue, a music critic, 'Beethoven's last quartets are mistakes, absurdities, the daydreams of a sick genius. . . I would burn everything I have composed if I ever wrote anything resembling such chaos.'[3] And on 6 February 1881 John Ruskin – himself a musical dilettante of the Mendelssohn school – wrote in a letter to his friend Dr John Brown: 'What you say of Turner is such a joy to me, but

Sinfonia grande

804 im bezpart
del Sig:

Louis van Beethoven

Sinfonie 3   Op: 55

how did you get to understand Beethoven? He always sounds to me like the upsetting of bags of nails, with here and there an also dropped hammer.'

Ironically, seeing that Beethoven had been planning to use this symphony as a calling card for his move to Paris, it seems not to have been performed in France until 1825 when it was cautiously given, together with the Seventh Symphony, in a private performance. Afterwards a member of the orchestra generously allowed that 'these two symphonies contained some tolerable passages; and that notwithstanding length, incoherence, and want of connection they were not unlikely to be effective'.[4]

In some ways it was the 'Eroica' that fixed the symphony as music's leading form in the nineteenth century. Its expansion of musical language – its fluidity of form, the stretching of the harmonically permissible with brutal dynamic contrasts – led inexorably to Wagner and the cementing of a kind of Teutonic hegemony over the century's musical taste. This was often fiercely opposed by composers of other nationalities (especially French), who found themselves comparatively helpless before the near-universal acceptance of German culture's brand of high moral seriousness as the *sine qua non* of 'proper' music. The self-proclaimed new style in which Beethoven had written the 'Eroica' was much later to be named his 'symphonic ideal', as will be seen in the next chapter. The imperious, buttonholing quality that made its first movement so impossible to ignore was exactly what some people disliked about the 'Eroica' and

The ceiling of the Eroica hall of the Lobkowitz Palace in Vienna. This was the Prince's private concert hall in which his orchestra held the first ragged rehearsals of the difficult new symphony that was dedicated to him. These took place in May and June of 1804 and the *Eroica*'s first full performance was probably given here on August 14 that year.

Beethoven's later symphonies, particularly the Fifth and the Ninth. They were all too clearly *public* music designed to sway and edify: arguably the earliest manifestation of a certain hectoring quality that was to become more evident in later Germanic symphonists such as Richard Strauss and Mahler ('Listen, damn you: this is serious! It's for your own good').

There was always opposition to this awed weightiness in France and Italy. Years ago at a concert in Florence I saw a programme note whose writer said the glory of Bach was that he committed one to nothing other than formal beauty, so it was hard to become bored with him, but that Beethoven demanded constant attention like 'a mutinous adolescent' – a phrase I have never forgotten. In the twentieth century, transatlantic musicians also managed slowly to haul themselves from beneath the stifling horse-blanket of the German classics. 'If I hear another bar of the "Eroica", I'll scream', Glenn Gould remarked when interviewing himself about Beethoven.[5] Elsewhere he described Beethoven as 'the one composer whose reputation is based entirely on gossip'.[6] He was more specific when singling out Beethoven's so-called 'middle period', which is usually dated as having begun immediately after the Heiligenstadt crisis. The 'Eroica' therefore qualifies as its first major work. 'In this period', Gould said,

Beethoven offered us the supreme historical example of a composer on an ego trip, a composer absolutely confident that whatever he did was justified simply because he did it. I don't know any other way to explain the predominance of those empty, banal, belligerent gestures that serve as his

themes in that middle period. . . All in all, I'd have to say that
Beethoven's most consistently excellent works are those from his early
period, before his hearing started to go – let's face it, that did affect his
later work – and before his ego took complete command.[7]

The contemporary American composer Ned Rorem makes no
bones about Beethoven being someone whose music he
simply doesn't need in the way that he needs French music,
despite having performed many of Beethoven's piano works
in public and ruefully conceding that he (together with
Schubert) is 'untouchable'. Untouchability, of course, is the
worst aspect of the Pantheon's fossilizing tendency in that it
leaves no real middle course between absolute acceptance and
absolute rejection. John Cage reportedly disliked Beethoven
while Michael Tippett was a devotee. Benjamin Britten
famously repudiated his early obsession with the composer,
saying in 1963, 'Sometimes I feel I have lost the point of what
he's up to. I heard recently the [last] Piano Sonata, Op. 111.
The sound of the variations was so grotesque I just couldn't
see what they were all about.'[8] This judgement makes Britten
sound indistinguishable from any of Beethoven's more
querulous Viennese critics a century and a half earlier.

Yet for certain contemporary composers Beethoven is a
figure to whom they find themselves returning. After taking
Beethoven somewhat for granted for much of his life, Harrison
Birtwistle has said:

Nowadays I have a completely different feeling about Beethoven, in a way I couldn't have felt in the past. He's a composer who never, ever, does what you expect him to. And what he does is never contrived. There's an early piano sonata – No. 11 [the B flat major, Op. 22, of 1800] – it's a bit like an embryonic 'Hammerklavier'. I thought it was extraordinary. In one sense you know the harmonic language but everything seemed new, as if for the first time. In some ways these thoughts [about Beethoven] have made me qualify my feelings about music I don't like. Or didn't like. Or didn't think I liked.[9]

Yet if Glenn Gould liked some of the early Beethoven (though the sonata Birtwistle singles out happens to be one that Gould particularly disparaged), there are modern musicians who find the late works indispensable. While conceding that Beethoven is not really a regular topic of conversation among his contemporaries, the composer Colin Matthews admits that 'they (like me) are likely to be drawn much more to the late sonatas and quartets than to the symphonies. The late works mean a great deal to me personally – and I don't think anyone writing quartets can possibly shut their ears to these so great works.'

That a modern composer can still experience this difficult music as a source of inspiration is surely an impressive indication of just how far ahead of his time the visionary old composer was. And not merely ahead of his time, either, but sometimes outside it altogether. If when you hear the slow, songlike theme that opens and closes the last movement of the E major Piano Sonata, Op. 109, the conviction suddenly comes that this is music for the end of the world, try to get your inner sceptic to refute the idea as fanciful. My guess is you will fail, and Beethoven's serene and weightless song really will be the one the world ends to: terminal stillness finally made audible.

8

THE SYMPHONIC IDEAL

Familiar as the 'Eroica' is (even over familiar), it is still easy to underestimate the symphony's sheer intellectual achievement and the shock it caused. Beethoven was quite aware of its greatness. Later in his life he admitted it was his favourite of all his symphonies. Back in 1805, regardless of whether they liked it or not, most people who heard its early performances in Vienna had to concede that it opened up new musical terrain. From then on the Beethoven symphony became a genre of its own, different in kind (and not merely in length) from its Classical predecessors. Yet the shock of the new prevented many from seeing how firmly rooted the 'Eroica' still was in traditional forms; and for the next century people would argue about whether it still qualified as a greatly expanded Classical symphony or was, on the other hand, the first example of a Romantic symphony. Beethoven's creative struggle from about 1800 onwards was increasingly concerned with *form*: specifically, with how to shape music – and especially a large-scale work such as a symphony – in a way that would retain its coherence while expressing something radically new and personal.

We now think of the high period of the Classical style that owed so much to sonata form as being that of Haydn, Mozart and the early Beethoven. Beethoven's 'early' period covers roughly the fifteen years between 1785 (the year of his three piano quartets when he was still fourteen) and 1800 when he was a lionized pianist–composer. At that time the compositions that most helped him make a name and a living remained

Giulietta, Countess Guicciardi, from an anonymous miniature on ivory that was found among Beethoven's belongings after his death. Society gossip in 1800–1 implied she was a notorious flirt. She became a student of Beethoven's and he evidently fell helplessly in love with her. It is likely that the very hopelessness of their social divide occasioned much of the despairing tone of the Heiligenstadt Testament in October 1802.

approachably within the late Classical style of Mozart and Haydn, such as his first and brilliant Op. 18 set of string quartets (1798–1800) and the tuneful if vapid 1799 Septet, Op. 20, a work Beethoven later came to loathe for its enduring popularity even though ironically it was probably his bestselling work in his own lifetime. By the same token his first two symphonies (1800–1802) and first three piano concertos (1795–1802) were well received. Still falling within the recognizable Classical confines in terms of their length and overall structure they nevertheless contained effects and ideas unconventional and daring enough to sound fresh and individual while not being too challenging for most listeners. Increasingly, though, Beethoven was dissatisfied with the limitations of the form he had inherited. It was obvious to him that Haydn and Mozart had reached independent pinnacles of perfection in their symphonies that effectively made their brands of orchestral sonata form something of a *ne plus ultra*, if not a dead end, even though dozens of lesser composers were still aspiring to that symphonic style. If Beethoven knew anything, he knew he was not a lesser composer.

The intellectual task he set himself was to work out a new and personal way of moving his music forward. Amid his popular compositions were already one or two that presaged a more radical style, especially the '*Grande Sonate Pathétique*' for piano, Op. 13 of 1797–8 that epitomized the stormy significance the key of C minor held for him. It still adhered largely to the basic structure of sonata form, but nobody else could possibly

have written it. The work's passionate nature established him in the Viennese press as a *Tonkünstler* or 'artist in sound', significantly a description Beethoven preferred to that of 'composer'.

Perhaps even more important to his stylistic development were the two Op. 27 piano sonatas (1800–1801). He described each as '*quasi una fantasia*', and there are few remnants of traditional sonata form in either. The second one in C sharp minor became known as the 'Moonlight' after the poet Ludwig Rellstab regrettably thought it conjured up 'a boat in moonlight'. This did wonders for the piece's celebrity while traducing the earnestness of the composer's intentions, which were surely not banally pictorial, for all the reflectiveness of the first movement and the passion of the last. The work seems to have been written under the influence of Beethoven's infatuation with a student of his, the seventeen-year-old Countess Julie Guicciardi. Certainly it was dedicated to her. Despite his occasional pretensions to having aristocratic blood (so much for his proclaimed egalitarianism: a legal case later in his life obliged him to admit that the 'van' in his name was not the equivalent of the German 'von'), Beethoven was a commoner. His passing passions for aristocratic women were never going to lead anywhere, but an implied romance with a young countess undoubtedly helped this sonata's nearly instant fame. Both its first movement, as well as the entire companion sonata in E flat major, have an improvisatory quality that Beethoven's contemporaries would have recognized from his

THE SYMPHONIC IDEAL

public performances but would not have expected in a published sonata. The 'Moonlight' in particular inhabited a dreamy musical realm no one had encountered before, and its first movement had the additional attraction that any amateur pianist could get his or her fingers around the notes and play it with suitably swooning demeanour. Not for nothing was this movement the party piece of E. F. Benson's fictional Lucia, endlessly performed for her variously fawning and catty listeners at one of her soirées in Riseholme. And, like Lucia herself, many an amateur has judiciously abandoned any attempt to play the much more demanding last movement within anyone's hearing.

By now Beethoven's attention was increasingly focused on giving his music motivic ideas that he could develop in various ways and make to bear cumulative significance. In orchestral music this could be achieved by assigning the motifs to different combinations of instruments at their various appearances, thereby casting them in new light, and by expanding them or otherwise altering them to release unsuspected potential. It was a method that, if handled skilfully, could give the music an overall sense of unity that the ear understood without knowing quite how. In this way individual ideas could be 'composed out' during the course of a movement or even over an entire symphony. It was this radical form of music that Beethoven perfected at a stroke in the 'Eroica'. The musicologists Joseph Kerman and Alan Tyson were to call it his 'symphonic ideal'.

OVERLEAF
The title page from the original edition of the piano score of *Wellington's Victory, or the Battle of Vittoria*, published by S. A. Steiner & Comp, Vienna.

WELLINGTONS SIEG
oder
Schlacht bey Vittoria

Für das Piano = Forte

von
Ludwig van Beethoven

91tes Werk.

— Eigenthum der Verleger. —

Wien im Verlag bey S. A. Steiner und Comp.

so wie auch zu haben:

in Leipzig bey Breitkopf und Härtel _ C.F. Peters _ Fr. Hoffmeister,

_ Simrock _ Offenbach, bey J. André _ Zürich, bey Nägeli & Comp. _ Ettwill, bey C. Zulehner, _ und in

gen zu Augsburg _ Berlin _ Braunschweig _ Frankfurth _ Hamburg _ München _ Mayland _ Neapel _ Stuttgardt.

Preis

The conception of this symphonic ideal, and the development of technical means to implement it, is probably Beethoven's greatest single achievement. It is par excellence a Romantic phenomenon, however 'Classical' one may wish to regard his purely musical procedures. It is also a feature that has offended certain critics, especially in the early part of the twentieth century, and set them against Beethoven. The composer himself was capable of producing a cynical and enormously popular travesty of his own symphonic ideal in the 'Battle Symphony' of 1813.[1]

The *Battle Symphony*, Op. 91, aka 'Wellington's Victory' or 'The Battle of Vittoria', was admittedly an aberration, although it was to bring Beethoven much needed money, exactly as he calculated. *Pace* the late scholars Kerman and Tyson, both of whom were lifelong academics on generous faculty salaries, it is not cynicism for an artist to scratch a living as best he may. Beethoven's *Battle Symphony* never infringed his symphonic ideal, because as 'characteristic' (i.e. programme) music involving cannonades and fanfares it was less a symphony than what today would be a film score, something along the lines of Tchaikovsky's celebrated *1812* overture. It told a story, dramatically and noisily, complete with national anthems. 'Battle' music had been a popular genre since at least the sixteenth century, and this whole period of wars and constantly clashing armies greatly revived it. The Bohemian composer Franz Kocžwara's *Battle of Prague* (1788) was written originally for piano trio, but in its piano solo version it went through dozens of editions pirated all over Europe and proving especially popular in England, where no salon or drawing room was without a copy. Beethoven's bid to cash in on this evergreen genre twenty-five years later was surely forgivable. Nor is it without interest. The hectic fugue with which it ends is not just accomplished writing but has pointers towards the Ninth Symphony. As Beethoven retorted to an adverse critic of the piece, 'I can shit better than you can write.'

Beethoven's 'symphonic ideal' is as good a name as any for the style of music he suddenly achieved with the 'Eroica'. It needs to be called something, if only to mark the gulf it instantly opened up between that work and every other symphony that had gone before it. It was not just a gulf of musical form, however; it suddenly introduced a dimension that even early audiences recognized as an almost *moral* quality. The music seemed to suggest to its listeners a narrative of high ethical struggle that ended in triumph. It was like an opera – indeed, a rescue opera – but one without singers or book.

It was small wonder that early listeners found the sheer originality of the new style bewildering. Some gave up on the spot, like the man at the symphony's first semi-public performance who shouted from the gallery in exasperation. Others no doubt struggled too but realized they were hearing a new and difficult kind of music with an energy that seemed to carry everything before it. And there was no doubt left in anyone's mind that this symphony's inner life was intensely personal. The hero of the piece might have been Napoleon, as apparently advertised; or it might have been the composer; or even some mystical fusion of them both; but the four move-ments recognizably carried the ennobling message of the

OVERLEAF
A page of sketched ideas for *Wellington's Victory, or the Battle of Vittoria*, Op. 91 (often known as the Battle Symphony). It celebrated a victory over Napoleon by the British in the Peninsular War. Beethoven originally wrote the second part in 1813 for a mechanical orchestra, the Panharmonicon, built by Johann Maelzel, the inventor of the metronome. In its full orchestral version it had a fabulous success in Vienna. Beethoven followed it with a piano version in 1816.

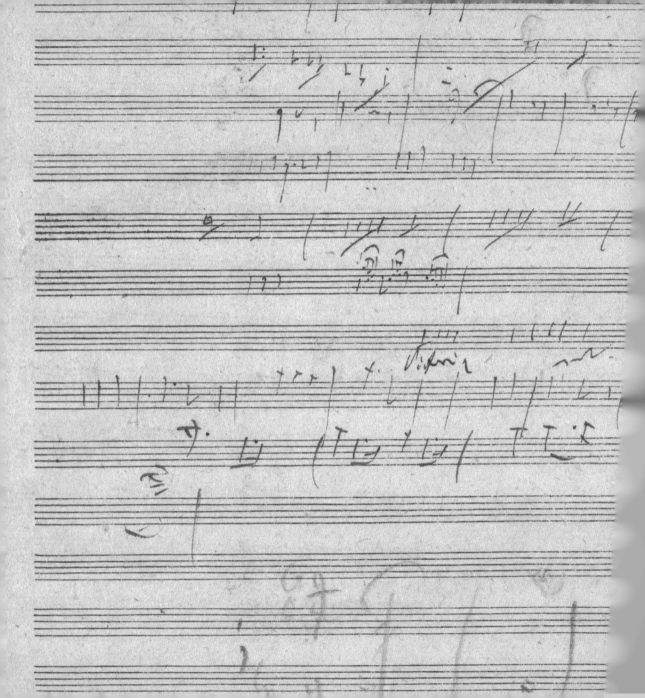

triumphant progress of a soul. This brand-new phenomenon of *nobility* in music was the symphonic ideal that Beethoven would carry through into his Fifth, Seventh and Ninth Symphonies especially. More than that, it was to lay the foundations of the symphony for the rest of the nineteenth century and even much of the twentieth as classical music's touchstone of high seriousness. It was no coincidence that Elgar's most characteristic musical marking was to be *nobilmente*. Soon orchestras were calling themselves *symphony* orchestras, and concert halls – especially in the United States – turned into symphony halls or even just 'The Symphony'.

Despite his 'new road', it was Beethoven's peculiar skill to retain as much of the Classical style in his music as he needed. In 1809, when his friend and patron Archduke Rudolph fled the French, together with most of Vienna's court, Beethoven wrote for him the Piano Sonata, Op. 81a, that became known as 'Lebewohl' or 'Les Adieux'. It is a very touching piece, straightforwardly programmatic, its three movements titled *Das Lebewohl* ('Farewell'), *Abwesenheit* ('Absence') and *Wiedersehn* [*sic*] ('Reunion'). The form of the first and last movements, oddly so for a middle-period Beethoven work, is of conventional sonata form complete with double bar-lines and repeats. The intensity of the sentiment is entirely his, especially in the bereft slow movement. Yet there is also a warm light-heartedness in the last movement that avoids the least hint of the sententious. All the same, by then a characteristic and essential ingredient of the Viennese Classical style was fast disappearing. This was the ability for music to be simultaneously intimate and amused. It had been one of the defining features of Haydn's string quartets: urbane, witty exchanges between the instruments as though they were old friends chatting in a coffee house. This sense of good-natured intimacy was one of the sadder casualties of the dawning Romantic age, as Charles Rosen lamented: 'The civilized gaiety of the classical period, perhaps already somewhat coarsened, makes its last appearances in the *Allegretto* of Beethoven's Eighth Symphony, and in some of the movements of the last quartets. After that, wit was swamped by sentiment.'[2]

There was even precedent within the secular Viennese classical tradition for including fugue in a symphony, as Beethoven did in the 'Eroica'. He was perfectly familiar with the last movement of Mozart's 'Jupiter' Symphony and was doubtless as astonished as anyone by the perfection of its coda, when the movement's four motifs or tunes are unexpectedly combined with each other while still making exhilarating music. Yet it was impossible not to feel that Mozart's display of sheer contrapuntal technique also included the faintest suspicion of 'showing off'. This element was completely foreign to the hard-won self-expression that preoccupied Beethoven and which is so apparent in the way he used fugue and other contrapuntal effects in the 'Eroica'. As with his sonata form, Beethoven's fugues were nothing if not personal. By the time he came to write the 'Eroica' he had mastered a counterpoint that could be successfully married to his symphonic ideal. Thereafter, the occasional fugues he incorporated into his music took on more and more of his personal voice until in the last movement of the 'Hammerklavier' Sonata as well as in the *Grosse Fuge* (the original last movement of the String Quartet in B flat major, Op. 130) Beethoven was producing fugal writing that could have been composed by no one else either before or since, so unique and powerful was the style. In such ways Beethoven made personal the various musical forms he had inherited. Even when he seemed to have abandoned them altogether they were usually present in spirit, bringing order to seemingly wilful disorder.

9

AFTER 'EROICA'

The French invasion of Austria in 1805 set in motion a social upheaval that in turn brought radical changes to Vienna's musical life. Many of the nobility fled the city, and the old eighteenth-century tradition of aristocratic patronage for composers rapidly began to dry up. It continued for Beethoven, but only because his isolation in deafness and his growing celebrity as Europe's foremost composer made it a matter of honour for his friends and remaining patrons to ensure his material well-being. Even so, at the end of his life his income derived more from publishers than from loyal supporters. Composers of a later generation such as Schubert, twenty-seven years his junior, found virtually no private patrons and were almost wholly dependent on commissions.

However, the collapse of noble patronage in the wake of the French occupation of Vienna did stimulate the founding in 1814 of the Gesellschaft der Musikfreunde, a society that sponsored true public concerts. This organization represented a definitive shift away from salon concerts and performances in the little theatres attached to private palaces. It was a trend that reflected Vienna's lively new social mix that in addition to the remnants of the aristocracy comprised a burgeoning middle-class audience plus the financial backing of wealthy bankers, mostly Jewish. In essence it was the shape that public music-making would take for almost the next century and a half, until in the aftermath of the Second World War European governments began using public taxes rather than private benefactors to sponsor their nations' music-making. In some

Beethoven lying dead: Joseph Danhauser's lithograph from his own drawing made on March 28 1827, two days after the composer's death and before souvenir hunters had bribed their way into the room to steal locks of his hair, leaving the corpse nearly bald.

cases (the Soviet Union, for example) this was Beethoven's youthful vision realized, of composers being paid by the state. On the other hand he would hardly have consented to the quid pro quo of being obliged to write only music that was approved by a regime.

Well before he died in 1827 Beethoven's music was out of fashion in Vienna – if, indeed, anything so avant garde had ever been truly fashionable. New styles had superseded it. Rossini took the city by storm in 1817 with the *Barber of Seville* and other tuneful, accessible operas. Weber's *Der Freischütz* followed in 1821 as the smash hit it had already been in Berlin a few months earlier. Then came a new generation of virtuoso instrumentalists. In 1828 Paganini's apparently superhuman command of the violin led impressionable people seriously to believe that he had made a pact with the devil. The showman in him astutely pandered to this by cultivating a Mephistophelian image, his skeletal frame clothed entirely in black. The following year Chopin came to Vienna with a dazzling piano technique, cutting such a romantic figure that ladies swooned and, when brought round, spoke of the unbearable longings his music aroused in them. Meanwhile Vienna's long love affair with dancing was being refined into the waltzes, quadrilles and polkas that the Strauss family and others would soon establish as the city's musical trademark.

By 1830 it was hard to believe that Beethoven had barely been dead three years: the transcendental seriousness of much of his late music seemed to belong to another era – many

thought to another planet. Yet over the years the Viennese public's attitude towards him had turned to affection. It increasingly mattered less that most would have listened to his later works such as the last piano sonatas and string quartets with bafflement. As the city's internationally renowned eccentric he had finally become a Viennese. Late in life he had even been imprisoned overnight as a drunken vagrant whose roaring protests that he was Beethoven were met with ribaldry by the policemen who failed to recognize him. (It is impossible not to recall the incident of the adolescent Beethoven furiously trying to rescue his reeling father Johann from arrest in Bonn.) By the time of his death Beethoven was eminent as well as unfashionable, both comic and tragic in true Viennese style. He was deemed fit to lie beside Haydn and Mozart – if only they could discover where Mozart lay, which to this day nobody ever has. Haydn had been buried some thirty miles from Vienna in the Esterházy-built Bergkirche in Eisenstadt, coincidentally the very church where in 1807 Beethoven had conducted the premiere of his Mass in C: an under-rehearsed and chaotic fiasco of a performance.

There was a huge turnout for Beethoven's cortège, the Viennese being fonder than most of a good funeral. Schools were closed, and many thousands of people lined the streets to watch his coffin carried to Währing church. After the high solemnity of the funeral service itself came the procession to the cemetery accompanied by the mournful sounds of a brass band in an arrangement of the slow movement of the A flat

Piano Sonata, Op. 26, that Beethoven himself had marked *Marcia funebre sulla morte d'un eroe*. It was notably not the *Funeral March* of the 'Eroica' they chose to play, but he was a hero nevertheless. At the cemetery they heard the actor Heinrich Anschütz deliver the playwright Franz Grillparzer's short oration outside the gates. Many in the crowds, sharing a sense of black humour, would have been amused had they known the extreme contrast between the solemn pageantry in its honour and the poor corpse the coffin hid. The boy from Bonn had made a dreadful death. His drink-abused liver had packed up and he had swollen grotesquely with dropsy. The liquid was tapped several times to give him some relief, the incisions for which (no anaesthetics or antiseptics in those days) had become infected and the wounds slowly poisoned him. Parts of Beethoven's body had begun to putrefy very noticeably even before death, and afterwards came the mutilations of doctors cutting out his aural organs to find the cause of his deafness and others eviscerating him to shake their heads over his liver. On top of that the cadaver was almost completely bald, so much of his hair having been cut off and sold to souvenir hunters.

Also unknown to the crowds, it would be Beethoven's posthumous fate to be dug up twice before being moved to Vienna's enormous Zentralfriedhof where today he lies beneath a copy of his original obelisk surrounded by other famous composers or else (as in Mozart's case) their memorials: the nearest thing to a musicians' Valhalla as can be found. In

OVERLEAF
Beethoven's immense funeral procession as recorded by Franz Stöber in a watercolour. The event was attended by an estimated 20,000 people, including Vienna's great and good. The bier was accompanied by the cream of the city's artists, including Hummel and Schubert (who would himself die the following year).

Thomas Hardy's epic verse drama about the Napoleonic era *The Dynasts*, Napoleon muses after Waterloo:

'Great men are meteors that consume themselves
To light the earth. This is my burnt-out hour.' [1]

Beethoven might equally well have said the same on his deathbed. Such is the passing of heroes.

The extraordinary art this hacked and rotting body had so lately produced and which has so deeply influenced people's minds for nearly two centuries still offers plentiful evidence of things not seen. Much of it has an unmistakably visionary quality, but a vision of what none can say. The cultural tyranny that Beethoven's odd-numbered symphonies in particular have imposed for the best part of two centuries is unfortunate if it has deterred a wider listening public from revelling in the exquisite balance and lyrical qualities of so many of his earlier works (for example, the Op. 18 string quartets or the 'Pastoral' Piano Sonata, Op. 28), as well as the sublime inscrutabilities of the last five string quartets, the last three piano sonatas, the *Diabelli Variations* for piano and, of course, the *Grosse Fuge*. Intended as the last movement of the Op. 130 string quartet, this work was deemed too knotty and unplayable at the time, and Beethoven instead substituted a more conventional finale. The *Grosse Fuge* went on to baffle the entire nineteenth century. It was seen as one of the Master's aberrations it was best to draw a veil over (like the *Battle Symphony*), and it was really only in the twentieth century that people began to come to terms with it. It was Stravinsky who famously described it as 'this absolutely contemporary piece of music that will be contemporary for ever'.

Each generation is newly uncertain that it has fully got to grips with Beethoven, and it might anyway now be impossible. Greatness has long since encased him like glass over a mantel clock, and, as Oscar Wilde once remarked to his friend Whistler, to be great is to be misunderstood. Much more recently the *New Yorker*'s music critic Alex Ross has wondered whether Beethoven can now ever escape the fate of 'monumental meaninglessness'.[2]

Even so, there were critics in his lifetime who claimed to understand his music. This is what the poet, artist and composer E. T. A. Hoffmann wrote in 1810 as a preliminary to reviewing a performance of Beethoven's Fifth Symphony:

Beethoven's instrumental music opens to us the realm of the monstrous and immeasurable. Glowing rays shoot through the deep night of this realm, and we sense giant shadows surging to and fro, closing in on us until they destroy us, but not the pain of unending longing in which every desire that has risen quickly in joyful tones sinks and expires. Only with this pain of love, hope, joy – which consumes but does not destroy, which would burst asunder our breasts with a mightily impassioned chord – we live on, enchanted seers of the ghostly world!
Beethoven's music wields the lever of fear, awe, horror, and pain, and it awakens that eternal longing that is the essence of the romantic. Thus he is a purely romantic composer, and if he has had less success with vocal music, is this because vocal music excludes the character of indefinite longing and represents the emotions, which come from the realm of the infinite, only by the definite affects of words?[3]

Beethoven thought very highly of Hoffmann's attribution of such transcendent emotionality to his music – as well he might, seeing himself enshrined in the same continuity of musical greats as Bach, Haydn and Mozart. More than that, though, Hoffman had described a heroic art that could exercise immense power over everyone who heard it. This it duly did, and with practical consequences.

By mid-Nineteenth century Beethoven's symphonies had become many orchestras' staple diet, the calorie-laden centrepieces of concerts in which new music from living composers often functioned more as *cuisine minceur*. It was Beethoven who did most to shape the future category of 'classical' music. Alex Ross has put this well.

In the course of the nineteenth century, dead composers began to crowd out the living on concert programmes, and a canon of masterpieces materialized with Beethoven front and centre. As the scholar William Weber has established,[4] this fetishizing of the past can be tracked with mathematical precision as a rising line on a graph. In Leipzig, for instance, the percentage of works by deceased composers went from 11 per cent in 1782 to 76 per cent in 1870. Weber sees an 1807 Leipzig performance of Beethoven's Third Symphony, the titanic, turbulent 'Eroica', as a turning point: the work was brought back a week later, 'by demand', taking a place of honour at the end of the programme.[5]

(Given that in 1807 Beethoven was still very much alive and would remain so for the next twenty years, Weber is presumably indicating that all trends must start well before they are recognized as such.)

It was the spiritual legacy of Beethoven's 'symphonic ideal' – the appeal to heroism and the brotherhood of man – that exercised an almost paralysing power over the future of much Western music. Had Beethoven fallen under a brewer's dray in 1802 it is debatable whether so many later composers would have felt obliged to choose the symphony as the vehicle for their grandest thoughts and likeliest bids for immortality. Those nine symphonies loomed their Parnassian bulk on his successors' horizons, their rarefied peaks glittering, at once unclimbable yet demanding to be tackled. Poor Brahms was practically paralysed by the awful anxiety of influence. He was forty-three before he summoned up the courage to write his first, very Beethovenian, symphony in 1876.

It is equally debatable whether the symphony as a form would ever have acquired the self-importance of sheer size favoured by certain late Romantic composers had not works such as the 'Eroica' and the Ninth greatly expanded the limits – both formal and aesthetic – of what a symphony might contain. Saint-Saëns's grandiose Third (1886), for example, has a prodigious finale with organ and two pianos. It is well written, of course: at once impressive and quite impossible to take seriously, being most easily read as camp parody. (Remember Berlioz's brilliant put-down of the young Saint-Saëns: 'He lacks inexperience.') In the symphonies of other composers it became apparent that the choral finale of Beethoven's Ninth had much to answer for. Mahler's Third, with its six movements, two choirs and average playing time of 1 hour 40 minutes, is probably the longest in the regular repertoire. His Eighth, the very epitome of gruelling high seriousness, is often called the 'Symphony of a Thousand', even though it generally scrapes by with a mere four hundred players and singers.

The idea that of all musical forms it was the symphony that might best express uttermost grandeur was no doubt behind Charles Ives's unfinished *Universe Symphony*. The composer described this as 'not music as such' but an attempt to depict the whole of Creation (a task Haydn had undertaken rather successfully way back in the 1790s). This has now been 'realized' from Ives's copious sketches and performed with his prescribed orchestra of 74 players, 14 of whom are percussionists. If it sounds like nothing on earth it must presumably meet the composer's original intentions.

It would be downright harsh to hold Beethoven in any way responsible for that behemoth of all symphonies, Havergal Brian's First. Known as the 'Gothic', it was written in 1919 and can last two or more hours by the clock or upwards of a week subjectively. It requires five choirs, solo singers and the biggest orchestra ever assembled. The percussion section alone calls for fifteen different kinds of instrument including a thunder machine and a bird-scarer. This writer was privileged (if that is the word) to have been at the premiere of the 'Gothic', given in 1966 in the Albert Hall under Sir Adrian Boult. It was an ordeal by decibels at the end of which the composer, aged ninety, made rickety bows to a cheering audience rendered ecstatic by sheer relief.

If the 'Eroica' established the symphony as a form of public music capable of exercising a kind of moral therapy and stimulating larger audiences to fill the new, purpose-built concert halls, it represented the democratization of 'serious' music, and it can be argued that this idea of music for the people had its roots in post-revolutionary France. Beethoven never made any bones about his music being designed for an audience far more global and enduring than that of a handful of Viennese princelings. In fact he was probably the first composer to be completely confident that his music would last. So it would not have surprised him that his highly political 'Eroica', as well as the Fifth and Ninth Symphonies, would be used promiscuously to set the tone of great national events. Between 1848 and 1849 his symphonies were played everywhere in the so-called 'People's Spring' series of uprisings in Europe. The 'Eroica' in particular was seen as enshrining the same spirit of heroic democracy that was inspiring new revolutions.

In 1880 the eminent conductor Hans von Bülow famously said, 'I believe in Bach the father, Beethoven the son and Brahms the Holy Ghost of music.' By the end of the nineteenth century Beethoven's music in general, but the symphonies in particular, managed to transcend even the use to which they were put to foster Teutonic nationalism. In the Second World War the Nazis cheerfully exploited Beethoven's music, just as the dot-dot-dot-dash opening of the Fifth Symphony was

read and used by the Allies as the Morse code letter 'V' for Victory, showing that Beethoven easily eclipsed mere German nationalism, his inspiration and recognition being universal. Later still, in this spirit the last movement of the Ninth has been shamelessly co-opted to serve as the European Union's 'national anthem', the 'Ode to Joy' turned into the theme song of a remarkably joyless institution.

Such is the universal fallout from a summer's work in an Austrian farmhouse over two hundred years ago.

A bronze bust of Beethoven by Franz Klein. It was based on the life-mask Klein had taken in 1812 so the composer's features are probably more accurately represented than in any portrait.

APPENDIX

CHAPTER 2, p. 23

The theme in the C major Piano Quartet WoO 36 referred to is practically a minor-key version of the 'Prometheus' tune. The rhythm is certainly right:

In the *Rondo* last movement of the Piano Quartet No. 2 in D major there is a hint of the same tune in embryonic form, now in a major key but in jaunty 6/8 time:

CHAPTER 5, p. 99

The reduced music score used here is Liszt's version of the 'Eroica' (he transcribed all Beethoven's symphonies for solo piano), and it is of interest that he was to use exactly the same device as Beethoven when in 1832 he sketched the opening of what was to be his first piano concerto – also in E flat – the only difference being that he went on to repeat it a step further downwards:

OVERLEAF
'Liszt at the piano': Joseph Danhauser's 1840 painting. Liszt may be the centre of his admirers' attention but it is clearly the over-lifesize bust of Beethoven that inspires him. The stormy sunset beyond the window suggests that the old composer has shown the way forward into the Romantic era. The figures (l. to r.) are Alexandre Dumas, Victor Hugo, George Sand, Paganini, Rossini, Liszt and the Countess Marie d'Agoult. The piano is by Conrad Graf.

Over these first two bars Liszt wrote *Das versteht ihr alle nicht, haha!* ('None of you will understand this' – the 'ha-ha' is sounded by the brass and winds where the strings have a rest in the second half of bar 2). It is very tempting to see this as a teasing homage to the 'Eroica' and the composer he most revered.

CHAPTER 5, p. 107
See Claude V. Palisca, 'French Revolutionary Models for Beethoven's *Eroica* Funeral March', in Ann Dhu Shapiro (ed.), *Music and Context* (Harvard University Press, 1985), p. 202.

a: Gossec, *Marche lugubre*

b: Beethoven, *Marcia funebre*

NOTES

2   THE BOY FROM BONN

1   Quoted in Marion M. Scott, *Beethoven* (J. M. Dent, 1951), p. 18.

2   Quoted in Joseph Kerman and Alan Tyson, *The New Grove Beethoven*, (Macmillan, 1987), p. 3.

3   Scott, pp. 22–3.

4   See Alexander L. Ringer, 'Clementi and the Eroica', *Musical Quarterly* 47/4 (October 1961).

5   Katharine Thomson, 'Mozart and Freemasonry', *Music and Letters* 57/1 (January 1976), p. 25.

6   Scott, p. 31.

7   H. C. Robbins Landon, *Beethoven: A Documentary Study* (Thames and Hudson, 1970), p. 57.

8   *Ludwig van Beethovens Stammbuch*, facsimile edition with comments by Dr Hans Gerstinger (Bielefeld-Leipzig, 1927).

3   VIENNA

1   Scott, p. 112.

2   See Fan S. Noli, *Beethoven and the French Revolution* (Tirana, 1991), p. 110.

3   H. C. Robbins Landon, *The Mozart Compendium* (Schirmer, 1990), p. 68.

4   'Verflucht, verdammt, vermaledeites, elendes Wienerpack!' (Letter to Joseph Carl Bernard, 15 September 1819).

5   'Elender Schuft und gemeiner Lumpenkerl!' (quoted in Noli, p. 92).

6   Anton Schindler, *Biography of Ludwig van Beethoven*, 2nd edition (Aschendorff, 1845), p. 56.

7   Noli, p. 77.

8   Jan Swafford, *Beethoven* (Faber & Faber, 2014), p. 204.

9   For a comprehensive collection of this music, see Constant Pierre *Musique des fêtes et cérémonies de la révolution française* (Paris, 1899).

10   Letter to Franz Anton Hoffmeister, 15 January 1801.

4   PROMETHEUS

1   Quoted in H. C. Robbins Landon, *Haydn: The Late Years, 1801–1809* (Thames & Hudson, 1977), p. 32.

2   Ibid., p. 33.

3   Slightly edited from Wayne M. Senner, *The Critical Reception of Beethoven's Compositions by his German Contemporaries* (University of Nebraska Press, 1999), pp. 190–95.

5   CONSTRUCTING A SYMPHONY

1   Hoffman, 'Beethoven's Instrumental-Musik', in *E. T. A. Hoffmanns sämtliche Werke*, vol. 1, edited by C. G. von Maassen, translated by Bryan R. Simms (G. Müller, 1908).

2   Scott, p. 99.

3   F. G. Wegeler and Ferdinand Ries, *Biographische Notizen* über *Beethoven* (K. Bädeker, Koblenz, 1838), pp. 77ff.

4   George Grove, *Beethoven and his Nine Symphonies* (Novello and Co., London, 1896), p. 77.

6   WHO WAS THE REAL HERO OF THE 'EROICA'?

1   John Clubbe, 'Beethoven, Byron, and Bonaparte' (n.d.), www.napoleon.org/en/reading_room/articles/files/clubbe_beethoven_byron.asp (accessed 27 April 2016).

2   Quoted in Maynard Solomon, *Beethoven* (Schirmer Trade Books, New York, 1998), p. 173.

3   See Peter Schleuning, *Beethoven 1800–1806* (Frankfurt/Main 1989), pp. 66–79.

4   Ibid.

5   Grove, p. 54

7   THE RECEPTION OF THE 'EROICA'

1   Scott, p. 52.

2   *Allgemeine musikalische Zeitung*, vol. VII (13 February 1805), p. 321.

3   Joseph d'Ortigue, 'George Onslow', *Révue de Paris*, 1ère série, LVI (Novembre 1833), p. 154.

4   Quoted in Grove, p. 93.

5   *The Glenn Gould Reader*, edited by Tim Page (Vintage, 1988), p. 50.

6   Quoted in Ned Rorem, *The Nantucket Diary* (North Point Press, 1987), p. 580.

7   Tim Page, *Music from the Road* (OUP, 1992), p. 102.

8   Murray Schafer, *British Composers in Interview* (Faber & Faber, 1963).

9   Harrison Birtwistle, *Wild Tracks*, edited by Fiona Maddocks (Faber & Faber, 2014), p. 21.

8   THE SYMPHONIC IDEAL

1   Kerman and Tyson, pp. 109–10.

2   Charles Rosen, *The Classical Style* (Faber & Faber, 1971), p. 98.

9   AFTER 'EROICA'

1   Thomas Hardy, *The Dynasts*, Part 3, Act Seven, Scene IX.

2   See Alex Ross, 'Deus ex Musica', *The New Yorker*, 20 October 2014.

3   Hoffmann, op. cit.

4   See William Weber, *The Great Transformation of Musical Taste: Concert Programming from Haydn to Brahms* (CUP, 2009).

5   Ross, op. cit.

INDEX

INDEX